I am incredibly thankful for this new book of poetry, prose, and drawing from the great Latino surrealist and one of the most generous and generative voices in poetry today, Roberto Harrison. In *Tropical Lung,* Harrison redoubles his commitment to sewing together the animal, the land, the human, the climate, and the technological. With sleight-of-hand and dense runic images, this book leads its reader into "the anti-silence of the Amazon" where we may just find a better way to belong. To think clearly in unclear sound is Harrison's persistent aspiration, and the addition of *Tropical Lung* to his rich body of work brings this aspiration closer to reality for all of us.

GABRIEL OJEDA-SAGUE
author of *Losing Miami*

Tropical Lung: exi(s)t(s) carries to us an urgent vision at the site of our survival, a symbolics whose operation is to unwork the racinated, dialectical, teleological, anthropocentric violences of the white colonization of the Americas that traumatically and destructively structure self-relation, community, and our ecologies. It dreams of survival not in a new world whose existence is founded upon mythologies of the absence of what was, but in a mind, neither old nor new, found in what has and continues to resist such erasure. To play the poems of *Tropical Lung* inside yourself, to ingest its program, is to open a promise that, like Macutté Mong who drew the colonizers' executionary axe from out of his head, we might "abolish the binary hatchet" disturbing ourselves and cultures towards destruction, and live instead in Mabila, in a "multiplicity of interface," in a posthuman imaginary, as Tecs in Tecumsah's republic. Roberto Harrison's recent books construct together a hugely ambitious visionary poetics of the Americas, and *Tropical Lung: exi(s)t(s)* is his most ambitious yet. I can't sufficiently stress how much we need what Harrison's writing dreams."

LEWIS FREEDMAN
author of *Residual Synonyms for the Name of God*

Roberto Harrison's *Tropical Lung* is a shock of breath in the hemispheric heat. Each word is a sleepless, gasping shadow of the metamorphoses happening in the poet's bones and the continent's convulsions. And all those shadows sink into the light of his relentless rhythm giving origin to words. *Tropical Lung* takes breath to the source of its origins in songs, dreams, star clusters, revolutions, and strokes of fiery color.

EDGAR GARCIA
author of *Skins of Columbus: A Dream Ethnography*

Roberto Harrison is a visionary. I mean he is one who sees beyond ordinary reality, and further he has the skill to transmit these visions—in *Tropical Lung* they appear as transmogrified psychedelia of the spirit, which is to say pure spirit, rendered through sweat and song and ceremony. They are gorgeous and astonishing, in all their animal, vegetable, cosmological, and mechanical forms, "within and after nature," all arising and hybridizing in a mixed futurity, which is also a past-present and a spacetime. He calls this the Tecumseh Republic, a place for harmony and "desirable dissonance," an earth-oriented society without borders: "the only viable future for the United States."

JULIAN TALAMANTEZ BROLASKI
author of *Of Mongrelitude*

Tropical Lung: exi(s)t(s)

Tropical Lung

exi(s)t(s)

ROBERTO HARRISON

OMNIDAWN
OAKLAND, CALIFORNIA
2021

Cover art by Roberto Harrison.
Front cover: *i sea words* (2020). Back cover: *interface password for faces* (2020)

Text set in Adobe Jensen and Scala sans

Cover and interior design by adam b. bohannon

Library of Congress Cataloging-in-Publication Data

Names: Harrison, Roberto, 1962- author.
Title: Tropical lung : exi(s)t(s) / Roberto Harrison.
Description: Oakland, California : Omnidawn, 2021. | Series: Tropical lung
  ; 1 | 'Tropical Lung' is a seven volume series of books. This volume,
  'Tropical Lung: exi(s)t(s)', is the first book. | Summary: "These are
  writings and drawings from and to a new homeland, a new homeland of
  Panamá that can be transmitted through the quantum martyrs beyond life
  and death, and/or a new homeland of the Tecumseh Republic, where
  technology grows to be necessary in understanding the ancient as well as
  then becoming erased and transcended by a now ever present electronic
  circle. It is a book brought close to the earth in its symbolic springs,
  to the light filled mystery that began with countering disassociation
  and by repairing a devastating explosion of interior structures
  necessary to being a person in the most foundational ways. It is where
  the screen removes itself by song as we move toward kinship beyond color
  mark"-- Provided by publisher.
Identifiers: LCCN 2021004833 | ISBN 9781632430892 (paperback)
Subjects: LCSH: Panama--Poetry. | LCGFT: Poetry. | Prose poems.
Classification: LCC PS3608.A78375 T76 2021 | DDC 811/.6--dc23
LC record available at https://lccn.loc.gov/2021004833

Published by Omnidawn Publishing, Oakland, California
www.omnidawn.com   (510) 237-5472
10 9 8 7 6 5 4 3 2 1

ISBN: 978-1-63243-089-2

for the prayer songs
for the fire
and for Brenda

"The stars will come out, what would be future is imperative,
what would be purification is only a song."

BERNADETTE MAYER

"moon
    arithmetic
      in the night
rain"

LARRY EIGNER

"Inner space is as infinitely explorable as spaces of the earth."

ÉDOUARD GLISSANT

"If, as Heraclitus wrote, 'Lightning creates the universe,' we can
perhaps say that the wound creates man."

EDMOND JABÈS

"He would never know what he knew. Such was his solitude."

BLANCHOT

"The thoughts of the night, always more brilliant, more
impersonal, more painful. Infinite pain and joy are constant,
and, at the same time, tranquility."

BLANCHOT

"Perhaps there is no return for anyone to a native land—only
field notes for its reinvention."

JAMES CLIFFORD

CONTENTS

LIST OF IMAGES

SOME INTRODUCTORY NOTES

Tropical Lung is a seven-volume series of books I am in the midst of writing. This volume, *Tropical Lung: exi(s)t(s)*, is the first book. I found the primary name after hearing once that there is an important *tropical lung* in the Darién jungle of Panamá, not far from Ciudad de Panamá, the city in which I spent some of my early years and where my family on both sides has been or been near for a long time. It seems to be common knowledge to me that a tropical lung is a dense place in the jungle that freshens the air, but somehow I don't find this on the Internet. I was born in Oregon to Panamanian parents who moved me back to Panamá when I was a few months old until we migrated permanently to the United States when I was seven. Spanish is my first language. I am the only one in my immediate family to be born in the United States and I am the only one who never wanted to be an American, not in any normative sense of the word, at least. I work to belong here as much as anyone, no matter what I choose to call myself, because I belong to the earth.

The final poem in my most recent book *Yaviza* (Atelos, 2017), is titled "tecumseh republic"—my name for a new post-racial, post-binary, post-apocalyptic, post-technology, post-colonial, holistically and earth oriented society organized around ontology and with no national borders, with Panamá as its only entry and its only exit, from a tall thin hill there where the air is more full than here. The Tecumseh Republic is formless and does not determine form or formlessness. It is named after the Shawnee Indian leader who tried to unite an Indian nation against racist Americans in the early eighteen hundreds. I pose the Tecumseh Republic as the only viable future for the United States. It will be something far beyond geography. A citizen of the Tecumseh Republic is a *Tec*. Tecs are endlessly proliferating instances of being(s). Tecs are texts too. The Tecumseh

Republic extends the possibilities of being human with the face and with the interface, further than what is possible with the face alone. Tecs first began appearing in this book. The images on the front cover and on the back cover of this book are both Tecs.

Mobilian is rooted in being a Tec. I am making something Mobilian through sevens in *Tropical Lung*. I first heard of Mobilian through the Hand Eye Symbolists who were everywhere in the Americas before contact. Mobilian is internal to *Mobilian Jargon*. Mobilian Jargon is where the Caribbean and Indigeneity are put together for harmony, desirable dissonance, and life. Mobilian is a language in internal life now as it was before. It is the language Tecs use to speak to each other and to work out the cultures and the possibilities of the Tecumseh Republic. Mobilian expands considerations of death, with death as more than nothing, with it also as a placeholder for counting and birth. By definition, Tecs spawn cultures in Mobilian by organizing around the main principle of generosity, not around greed.

Tecs are becoming more and more cogent and fluent as collectives. They know the lines, forms, colors and their solitudes, they see by the fire of the symbols planted by speechless ecologies. The foundation of the Tecumseh Republic has as its key the option or a way for and toward Indigeneity for color. At least in terms of the new and the still to be reflected upon by the Start, at least to make a good space for the future for those of us who want to navigate in this way. I mean the earth. But this is just a Start and an end to computation. Especially now with the return of the circle on many of our screens and the new realities made by the weather and by the qubit. And now by COVID-19. I mean the earth.

I take a pre-historical period, with Mobilian rooted in the Mississippi Era, if only because I have dream ancestry there in some way, in a log that sprouts books through a river of terror and allows us to cross without symbols or signs. Mobilian is how Mabila lays the groundwork for the Tecumseh Republic and makes the Tec possible, even as the Tecumseh Republic has no form. Mabila is a source of psychic and symbolic mixture here from the beginning of counting. I have sometimes seen it as a psychic and symbolic origin of mestizaje for fours. Only the music knows for sure and only it can open the door. Mabila flows color and raises the line for relation with and through Panamá for the Tecumseh Republic.

I use Saloma (https://youtu.be/fzCdy9PfonE) ways of reflection between face and interface, and between outer faces and inner faces, to make Tecs now. Tecs are born in silence and return to the silence past what is seen. Silence is where I am from. If I reach silence in reading a poem I wrote or in making a drawing of a Tec, which becomes the being(s) of a Tec, it becomes something that I can belong with. Thus we come to the first meadow → The weather reads me this way . . . I am the husk and the dead leaves past winter that send out signs, symbols, and songs. A true and natural Mystery precedes me. I am within and after nature. Nature is within and after me.

Mobilian is how I trace mestizaje through to Indigeneity and put them together as sign and symbol. Mabila is a place to be. The songs that relate us come from the fire. I read the patterns in the rites of countless corn fields and in the skins of the snakes that inhabit them. Do genes imply these ways? Or must it be history united with kinship and songs? *Tropical Lung: exi(s)t(s)* revolves around a drum, the songs sung on the drum, and the sweat lodge. One of the main events in the book is the attempted execution of Macutté Mong (Black Loon*), a young Ottawa leader in Michigan in the early eighteen hundreds. An American officer attempted to execute Macutté Mong with an axe (or a tomahawk), to which he responded by pulling the axe out of his head and handing it back to the officer, not once, but three times. I see this as a symbolic moment in history pregnant with meaning. It rejects a rigid, Western, binary mind imposed upon the Americas. Forever. In *Tropical*

* Thank you to Mike Zimmerman, Jr. and Jay Sam for the translation.

Lung Macutté Mong escapes after handing back the axe the first time. He then heals up the palms of the Hand Eye Symbolists of Panamá in the waters of the Mississippi. He as they makes us see again beyond survival, as a Host of survivance.

I have been active in the Indian community of Milwaukee for over ten years. I participate in the sweat lodge ceremonies at the Indian Community School here as well as on the Oneida Indian reservation near Green Bay, Wisconsin. David Powless organizes these sweats and sings most of the prayer songs in these ceremonies. David's prayer songs are the most powerful prayers I have ever heard. I was in a drum circle informally with David and other friends for several years as well at the Gerald L. Ignace Indian Health Center on Mitchell Street here. I have done the smudging and a four directions prayer at the Lutheran Church of the Great Spirit for many years. The Four Directions Prayer at Great Spirit is the most beautiful prayer I have ever read. I do not consider myself Lutheran or Christian per se, but I do believe in the higher unity of all spiritual paths. I don't know much about Indian ways. I don't know much about Panamanian ways either, though I am Panamanian. And I am dark to myself. In some sense I am a religious writer without religion. I bring the near to the far. I go to where there is no sign to the other side of muteness. I am a knowledge worker of absence. Great Spirit values what I bring. They see it as Indian. Not Oneida, not Ojibwe, not of any other tribe, but as Indian. Sometimes as Panamanian. And sometimes Panamá means nothing to me except that I am alone. Sometimes it means everything. That I am alone. Then there is everything in between. Panamá. I have others now. And after COVID-19?

Tecs find silence at the center of the earth in Mobilian Hosts. The fire through suffering brings us close to the earth with the Tecs, with our songs and the links to the stars through the wood. Red and black clusters move through the fires in the Tecs. I love Great Spirit and I love our lodge. These are two distinct and related communities. I have learned so much in being a quiet part of things there. I have learned from other spiritual communities too. But I don't belong in those communities the way I do at Great Spirit and in our lodge. Often, a place of silence in them is a place of silence in me. I have always thought of myself as an Indigenous person. I am one and I am not, together. What have I lost from Panamá that leads me here? Or what do I have? What does a person need in order to wander? A future knowledge shatters the Red Oak on a split horizon. We travel in seed husks as we enter with Spring and hatch from underground. Tecs put the circles together through music. They give me a place to belong outside, outside of the isthmus. I make as I wander past death and computer trash. I am a spark in the fires of the ancient worlds of the Americas now. Texts make Tecs to be seen. And Tecs make texts to be heard in blind silence. I went on for years after I left the old shells and found them again as containers for Starting.

I start with seven and I end with four.

But I know nothing. I always know nothing. And so I am always new to the world. Even to the worlds where I might belong.

Tropical Lung: *exi(s)t(s)*

a new break of the body

the pages of a tree

fold a people's star into the lower
swarm releases. others move light in their sewn

connections

a window to the body burns
as one is dead in two. as the in-between colors
do not rest as the shoulders do, toward the East

the paper dissolves. with no retrial, the approaching road
to the Sea is written

she does not have the magnet. they return
to make monuments

of the sounds of action

through the door. when the option to dress
makes the swarm return to the embrace

of the disappeared, the more dissolving
lines remain past what the water

moves to retrieve

inconceivable islands
of synthetic meat

identity marker for the animal light (mixed seed)

there is nothing
by the door. light finishes

the interior animal
moves with a warm

night. no eclipse
makes the uncooked fright of the bodies

see with a straight line
to the Face   reflective

       coats heat after
       mineral
       escapes. push

    to remain in the show
    of distances.

    death invites . . .

what is the air

    module

through the red and black sound?

destroyed by the screen

a new person undoes the efforts of the Sea. we do not Start by the ashes
as they attend to the shadows and pull back the ghosts to wear the flesh
      by night

their open return to the empty navigations carves the island weather. it is dressed
      in shells.
but they do not pile up the wounds of the approaching split and cracked
      interiors

where someone reveals the path to the face as the secrets protect an Oceanic
      blood
from nothing, and the herds of giants relay to demolish the interfacial
      recursions

of leaves. there are no doors to the exit full of exiles, of the incoming wound
retained for Islam, as the spinning horse attends to the increasing options of
      collapse

and someone does not see their own evil, as one does not improve to the
      number net
by the arriving winter. their origins are vast again

like the soil of the engorging
packet

transmission. death is my pupils
large and small through the burning echoes

interface

I intend and abandon the storms that surface out of your facial reconciliation targets. By the fire here there sit the dividing lashes of the mote discoveries as they promise that the surface of your eyes collects the rust from the earth to exteriorize the wound of the first animal color. The night follows beyond what might restart the sand detection of the Sea. Someone detaches the sky's knotted hoops to remove the ear that unravels the disconnections outside. The disappearing processor draws eggs into the surface of a black kite with those feelings made for the light as it links the animals back to the ferns. After that there is nothing to divide what might dissolve into fine catacombs and the season, with its negated services, resolves to remove my background agents. As the increasing likelihood of my disaster recedes, the night decides the approach to the rainbow by the work of the dusters and how they revolve to infuse the bird sounds of the summer with blood, as they fall to the beginning territory of the tapirs one approaches the thrice nonexistent sweat of the desert for the first and last mound.

toward a tropical lung

four magnets
populate
the land shadows
as the network
displays the reflected solution
to packet the light between us
and dissolve the pronouncing tide
as a tunnel to the night

Yes, because something tears the train from the interior electric loops
and the earth becomes more automatic and increases the hidden waters.
There is a net blank that the power of the button does not allow in the
competitors of color. And while thought is not attached, only the slight
can hear the music well. When one of us leaves to belong to the sounds
of the web we also become less measurable in pictures. The window goes
out of town and shatters on the other side of el borrado ser humano.
We walk slowly to undo the attachment service of the name protection
team and then the horses wander softly through our comfort. Someone
is standing in the midnight slot but we are using the same pen for the
morning alarm. Each service train sews us to the chest and we become
the solitude of flannel. When they fight for the stupid they also fall past
the earth and into the distant boundary line of the clouds. They read
them, those clouds at the surface of my stretchable heart space, but the
morning also does not appear to the fragments of reflection. When
they are accused of terror, they are also put down as softness by the
recognition Sea. A subset of time cannot be the book offering to the
Aubrey Williams Hymn to the Sun of the Olmec and Maya nascent with
its seed solutions. Death smiles easily in the electronic womb.

borrado ser humano

The opposing vestibule remains dear to the hidden exception of the gnat, as more guns return to the harvest of the blind ash and its blessing. Another fold appears to remove the light contusions and some become the outside visitation of the pulse beyond music. It is there that the opening aggressions resume to be the twelfth red and black sound. Within the cloud negating Sea it resets the triplet's inception to the middle ground. Or she or he removes the increasing dust to the goat of disturbances. Function does not water the soil for the buttons, and the instruction is met with pure vacancy in the wandering fish. Without the receptacle of the electronic mute we dissolve to find less number for the story. The bison attaches itself to the projected night and sees within the interrogation dismemberment team. And she of the cyclone circle removes the bottle from the weeks long slow decapitation of each continental mirror. Now that we see ourselves in the nowhere map we are more alight to a world without reflection. The final gaze burns to the ground to give us the most pure golden disc of the image. She calls and she calls el borrado ser humano to expire her coercion in a cyclone of intention. The dreams of the second stone respond with a quadrant stagger by this side of the Darién jungle. They sit still for the tiny and colorful poison frogs. Down by the Sea we absorb the Dolphin Zeros through our body light regions and flood our first memories with the origins of both suffering and pleasure.

middle ground

an organic function of escape
chairs and stones on the surface
pierced and disproportional symbols
release the heat storm of the offering
to palm out the lung restitutions
in the hidden wombs
and their mystery silences
from the bone window interface. escaleras
simbólicas de los borrados

escaleras simbólicas de los borrados

We become the line as we absorb the blood and parts of a morning's climate. After the show there are three moves that capitulate to the undersea robotic logins. The machines call us less than silence. When the afterimage endures through our swarming conversations the only night sky punctured with reading projectiles removes the people who cannot answer. When the float of the water and the swing form contusions they slow down our protests. When the placid of the night do not push the language from the team we deploy the Host and start at the war of plants, the war herb symbol of a Black Elk rumor. Each intentional exit dissolves as each word is spoken. Even when the firing table does not reveal the beginnings of the symbol, even then we do not stand inside the weather. The rain drops the summer and we end up having to hold it up ourselves. People are without wood and so they starve for a table without the Earth. We deploy the end of the number to make our hands write.

When each person does not know the way to start we are left without the webbing science of the knot. In the outside there is not one line to see. Out of our open memory we die from the background of beginning. Each life is like that, without a day to unravel or stream. But when most of us disappear we begin the language. Each of our service animals desires what we do not know. But then the equation belongs to accept again and the circles cut our skin. In the outdoor seating we explain that one of us is not the foundation of the paper night. And we cut the line to explain that those were standing. Even if the explanation cannot relax my throat, the signs of the country make sounds that terrify each organ. Are they just sounds? Why fear the violence that surrounds us if our music cannot explain? Which of our empty torsos can become us to endure the approaching winter? Even if no one hears, we are listening to the last sounds of the age and we are seeing the fire to come and bloat us in the heat. Our empty words are not soft. They punch a hole in the screen. And where does it end now that it has begun? Which body should I endure to be like the Self() of the canceled? How many faces can I believe with my senses? What Self() interface works for you?

hand writing ocean sea ocean

33

symbolic philosophy

I scar up the final exterior side of my shadow. Some see set groups on my skin as the star of redemption delays its dream pierced releases. When the rings of the animals wade into water and send me the snow, I attend to the solvent for words and the cage of our science returns what the news leaves behind. In explosions of power the lucid rehearse their last mornings and send out the moss that their minds do not see by the orbital water. The water returns to the engine of sorrow as death leaves me fresh by the withering fruit and I walk to the door that's been open since birth. Through there I announce that the thinking has stopped by the ink and that words do not stick to the screen anymore, as we listen to know what the pulse of our Oceans will follow with light and the animal souls. I see violence delay its own death by the slough of a snake. I bring out the relative rocks in the protest of shapes. I sing like archaic designs for the marrow. Their shadows remember the Host as it teaches the tongues to split sounds and the persons inside. When someone projects me I shrivel to sand and pronounce every shore by the jungle. When they call me by staring and hang by my limbs every night I propel my aphasia and erase every book to replace them with drawings and symbols of mud.

When I as a suture get death in the morning, it revolves for the shattering puncture of faces and pummels the orange with Sea and the Oceans of transposing silence. The night does not cut me as knives sink their way into pools of the network of vision which hungers for Starts in the symbols and moves every number of weather with trees. As the surface of unity crumbles to let in the Host, I remove the attention of heightened design and protect the beneficent beings with shelter in many. But One does not stop at the face-to-face mode where the other dimension of fire sinks down to the multiple underground layers and softens the wings of each bird. As the eagle flies higher than storms and burns off hir face and hir tail with the fire of inception, we transport every tapir of tropical insight from silence to Float. Then silence transforms the sparse willows inside every speaking as monuments pulse with dissolving and carry out songs for the throat. Each evening dissolves and removes the earth's patterns like a panther's third dream of shape four and shape seven for shelters of color to breathe with old songs. Then after the functional heartache a cloud builds the symbol farm ready to fill up the stones with the heat of each feather, each charging relation of horses and bison made light by the tiny bright frogs of our home. Their colorful poison remembers the shadows for modules recursively built in the snow. Once corn builds the creek we align with the toucan to harvest the path with the data from finishing books to the skin. From there we use hands for the shelter of promising storms and relay every message from cracks in the parallel roads for the boat.

transposing silence

When morning sends time to the networks of shadows laid out to arrange the first travels of light through the snow, the micro adorned and the ossified colors of seeable nights renew their contractions of circles to move with the beat of a drum. As horses rush over the segmented spirit of technical sparks, the deserts dissolve to make room for the cracks in the bombs that read for the numbers and fall for the line. As networks replace the in-motion desiring lungs and the bloom of explosions the other worlds send us, the rocks of the ground now have memories paved for the tongue. They speak and they sing of the penetrant cycles of greed and of lessons that tear at the fabric of heart cut response. As cumulative handles through days and reposing send arrows in session that pierce through the smoke of each gun, their magnified steps and their isolate scorn for the orange remains to undo the intention of robots to stand for the button and cut with a worm what belongs to the night. If hassles like radio servants and workers for digits remember their exits to ride with the Sea, a memory effort of symbols that raid with a war will never return as four bodies are forced into knots of eight parallel tombs. With Spring the attention to wearing the cut for the filter of borrowing stones moves colors to rein in the shadow and bloom with the vent of directions to find the best zero of origin worn to the ground. Something as someone responds to the promise of night works and sees what the rain in the shallows redo the sharp waves in the air with. A memory riots descriptions of dreams, the dreams themselves wander through openings made in the morning to carve a world in. I split in my wandering hollows and whisper the truth of the worlds in each muted connection of motion and rest in a space as the moorings of all those that like to push hassles and die with a silence in Seas as they do for the teams in a fuse. With patterns of backgrounds announcing the color of blood, I push out what the racist reveals to be short for his face.

When windows stack sunlight and shelter the motes of direction we make in the tunnels through frozen recessions of plants that the tapirs make homes in and seek out the Host for the dunes of flesh circuits for many remains by the colors of fire and the hardest wood let in for Seas as the air comes straight in and doubles the soil. The circuits maintain what the serpent designs in the midnight of working out shapes and the numbers for time that the road weaves its ground in to demonstrate bodies for red and black sounds as a motion for lions in Florida as pythons return to the cracks. Even if sounds do not sharpen the evil fit lines of the mounds, or if lines turn to stations of light, their family harmony losses will vacate the integer lessons of zero and one for the quantum and whole by the peaks for the conjugal lakes. As penetrant staples relay their most virulent racial attire, the eggs of the ground will not go as she fills up with songs for cold exile and lies under sacral revisions and moons. She forgets to remember the number that race made for seven as moss grows to shatter her matches of face-to-face shells that the earth moves within. He makes animals wander and speak by the segments of radio plays to the zeros of birth. They put it all on in resembling the witness that sides with the symbols that float through the countries of night and dissolve to make knowledge a fluid invention of seven, with four making eons their patterns of cyclical pasts in the stories that plug into faces and move with the wind.

The clock makes the nectar of pus be the mode of reprisal for sugar and smoke from cigars through the islands of vision and improvised bodies alone in Milwaukee where burials hatch out the moments of trouble in husks of mamones that litter the streets with my destinies here in the snow. Without bodies the wars of the screen steel connection from skinless street zombies and motions that tear at the Hosts of the corn as the meteor sends us to shivers of glass and the gloat of the suffering ants with their infinite lesions retake with the house that is straw for the storm and the Start of the tracks by the Sea. The body inviolate tears off into stillness inanimate portions and quivering animate steps as dimension explodes to increase the Heaps through the surfaces following sunlight and moonlight through terror and earth by the Sea. If we die in one angle and sink by the letters pronouncing the sleepless interrogate caption by profiles within the more cognitive blocks that the opened up flower reveals to be deathless alone as the plant of the morning, we turn through the closing dimension for space and a network of trees and proceed. As the heart stays in shadows where others pronounce the arrival of animals out of Darién, they weep and link up to the giants of weaponized clouds that Start with the Host of the deer and the penetrant cycles of movements where parrots in linked up alignments remove the attachment to Season in stocks for the Milky Way in the last drum. Shape keeps the marbles inside the detachment of honoring earth in the Moundville inside the obsidian Ocean to birth with the meat. With reticent cycles of hatred the redness of moorings in swamplands of pus make the trudging to refuge in parts of the symbol of landscape a part of the symbol of sky by the saltwater keys of the radio spent for the heat, to bring back our nation of stars. Again and again we mirror the face-to-face captives who slide out the natal response to the pulse of the Sea and come to the patterns of AND that return what the native of hearts brings us out for our suturing needs through the sweat and to see.

i was sewn

The body is sliced into regions where worlds that will differ pronounce and proceed to speak nets through the tunnels that reach different numbers, foundations of being, returning the Host to be origins saddled to rise with twelve altar dimensions turned in to the segments of time in percussive relations made simple by work in plantations remembered outside the allotment of weed for the water war memory saves. The bodies of color with severing speech reach the mountains escaping the need to belong to the binary fitness resolved by the centuries filled up with death to remember it now for dismembering wildlife projections hidden in snow. Three hemispheres fall into place for the offering mornings cut into with sevens for breaking the chain of oppression and network relations bloated along the cold rivers fit still to return to the light. The oxygen makers and animal people resume by the zero inside the intention of swelling the patterns considered for ashes returning the sacral recession by thieves. If she is the every repeated dimension in travel for history's shape by the spiraling mouths, then seeds for the breaking through rooms in the white of deception remove the acceptance in tools as the impetus marking the homeland with eggs and the doors of the tombs. If seals in the vacuums of faces receive the last message of Mounds to the future of sorrow and red for conjunctions, the corn flake of death returns winter with wisdom replaced by the engine of letter shaped proofs. As the planets shrink down to the cells in the yellowing spirits, the animal memories attached to the organs that swell up the night with extended escapes marking each of the palms with the passwords to freedom and spinning black circles of mud come to be. Conflict returns to the meadow to see with the promise of action resuming the destiny carved for the anti-aligned El Dorado in twisting inanimate persons attached to the secretive organs and wandering plants. I release all the locks that I find in the Ocean and see with connection removed for the light of communion with trees.

When the opening out to the semblance of neural design and the providence gated to make the first outing a promise to feed the aligned with the charge of the sun runs the arrows to burn up the salt in the ocean, I magnify circles in mouths to believe. The wild ones resume in the scrolling attachments their own ample death in the eggs that the counter resends to the target that bleeds. They call me to winter the summer with blankets and thunder outside the protectorate rattled in languages meant for the Sun. Even if tribal ascension marks chain breaker children with knives in the hope that derives from the Sea, I accept that the marker removed for the souls of the insects returns our Bolivian files for infusions of tropical sight. The white is disease for corrupting the sand and the ferns with our stories split up in their veins, their memories shoot for the fire and recede. Attacks from the partial inanimate movements center interior exits and serve to remain by the hulk of the problem they circle their Start by the light of design and defend all the weakening silence to hollow the force of the ferns. They packet the sheltering storms by the cognizant rivers and burn off the whiteness to feed with the absence of red and black suns. As the ground swells the offers of science in destiny marked by the palms, their origins startle the welcoming flight of the cat and remove the forgetful displacement of time seeds to move with the sand. I argue that madness has stars by the color of radiant blackness and tunnels to feed with the wind. Without the pronouncement the book marks the cover to skinless recessions and links to the organs outside in the sky. Many will follow the form of the opening death to the death that is promised for leaves by the end of the meat. And some will retry by the slingshots that bloody the hand for the sleep in the straw in the dreams that repeat.

grandfather stones

Death marks its season with doors that I give out in patterns replacing the snow. The doors Start invisible entries and exits with skinless stiff bodies of alternate windowless people wandering home. If exile makes sense to the number as color reveals its intention to breathe, then the doors quickly open and close as they hold me with fire and the animals seethe. Without the last layer of skin to appeal to the lust of the gadget, I harbor the storms of the throat and deny all the paths that the others repeat in the colors of blindness. Some of us see that the door winds itself into death as four pages are written in blood, and as I am the first and the last in the middle to stop the machine with a mark. There is no longer a way for connection to harvest its thrills by the windowless voyage of psychic and integral wounds to retrace the allure of the Sea. Many more axes and shelters sink in to the fractals that curve in Caribbean zeros sent into the past and the future of night. As mornings replace the psychotic inception of value, we give dreams to the semblance of teams with the move that I peel. As I number the seven replacements of evil and the four other sides to the heat, the bodies of humans with animal heads mark the first to begin on the feet by the leaves far away. No one replays in the ashes a wandering hand that makes number for night. I as the Sea in a stone mark the weather to make us return to the islands and count to the music that startles the tapir with Starts of the bison for four of our yesterday's tracks. Nothing remembers the zero to be with a one as I stop for the death of this day with a page.

The starving allotment of grasses and daylight makes night be the service that patterns retain by the force of the shells that unravel for songs. They move by the window that heats up the hands of the rent by the bodies attached to each face for alarms. Without the round sessions, the answer to light heated symbols of traction replace what the questions sit down with to bring out the seals in the hidden equations of color and marks by the faces that leak in their prison deletion escapes. The harvest of digits and forces retain what the mention of cotton replays in the rhythms parked in to the Start of the storms. With markets replaced by the rinse of the trees and the hawks in their shelters, the shepherds return to the secrets of dogs by the feet of each circle and turn. The void then retains what the borrowing sack by the child in the cages reveals to be pregnant for rain and the packets of signals to night in the shadowy stripes of the day. The weakened reception of giant and tropical leaves from the Start makes the origin stories of vastness close to the throat. They settle for dust by the husk wrenching stones that become like the life of the children now ready to sing with a drum and the nation of stars by the seven that captures the bear. With song the increasing inception of chain breaking tongues marks the ready black road of the underground notes of the promise that keeps all the rocks seen alive. In separate intentions the forces of persons made other by light in their algebra groups and topology facets a stretch beyond one in the future of hives in the heart as a shape that makes others return.

Time weaves its wounds past the body in twelve different places dismembered to move with the worlds left behind. Each part of its army of pieces remakes what the heartless inception of forms turns from shape to the doors of the wombs. Their red and black cycles are fated as music defends them to send out a key for the cages of mental contusions in artifice shed by tyrannical tears. But the real makes hir shadow a harvest by putrid alignments from cattail to memories slashed by the knife. Blood marks its shepherd to wade into Oceans made red by the weeping retention of occupied leaks. Dispersal reveals the lead bottom of hearts marked by bombs in a lie of recursive connections for serial memory faded to speak for the accent of hanging the moon. The marriage of feet by the teams of recession and neutral delays in communicant infants returns as a sweat to the cycles of color and sutures begin to unravel the seven for one. He magnifies operant harvests of partial responses to wisdom suggestions that mark up hir citizen points and destroy the paternal repression by plants making fewer thick modes. No refuge as missiles shoot out of hir baby alignments and crush my reception of signals made light for the dark. Even if lessons resume by their memories frozen to empty warm lakes and make eves for the Sort, she marks what her castle dissolves to redo a way out. If solitude rings in the earth she may see that the stitches that harbor the road to a tree make more rapid alignments to number the residents able to sing. And often the powers that stabilize artful escapes to the wind where the animals rescue the fire – that I am without—from a Self()—and am cut out to walk through the door. Those fires are the sharpened refrains that they as the animal stories repeat and consume by archaic dimensions of night that the stars leave behind – as they move to become us again. Now that the whiteness of sale up in binary problems has shown us an evil to be the control and the punishing life, I as they stand as the qubits to bring what the power delays. The bodies we move are not there and neither am I for the now—or for time gone below—or even for morning tomorrow—as timber like patterns map out a new face and we swarm.

refuge

tec knowledge

infinite shifting is at the forefront
of the speech of the palm trees
in the womb collapsed by signs. the ship
plows through each donkey's artificial pointers
as we wander the slope to the flower
and orient the faces of the night. speaking
is silent by the continental Mound
as the flies float up
past the desert surfaces
of our longing to be
objects of catastrophe. things
speak their own languages and reflect
past our origins, as they pull
it all behind the screen,
to canoe the electrified—nothing
survives. all of life
looks to the screen to cross the neutral,
the psychic knots stay behind us
as death proceeds

i am not the light, i do not exchange
electrons with your bodies. i escape
and call you to return
to the fire to begin. we receive the visions . . .
all is born in the anti-silence of the Amazon,
as we mold the divine
and the giant leaves and the long necks
call us to be true
to the arrow → she teaches us
to walk the red and the black

and to make Saloma
the future of the ancient hollows
and documents
with a Start at Mabila
between everything

the rabbits of the rabbis
in the caves of Spain
become the smoke
at Pipestone

the maiden semblance without eyes
tastes the fold of death
and makes the buffalo born

every city
of Mounds

every twilight
every sphere of night

brings us the circles
to see seven

i sing for the sun
i am born
in the stars
i have no light of my own
and i abide because of the mystery

and dissolve
our lunar life

native reversal

what brings me to share that the train
fails to compromise the shadows, that the Sea
will not return my hunting? with the colors
of the plants I embrace
the extinguished exceptions, the adorned
monuments raised to the ampersand quality
of the ground. I was not here
to receive or to see the skin planted origins
as I move through the protections
of the starlight, which now
abandon my face. I was not one
by the music which shatters
the morning. I am not the vision
that you feel by the mute, as I
have contorted my own
two tongues for the Sea. without hope, I
continue to dissolve past my future
arrivals to an Indian god, and I return
my palms to the horses as they run
out of food. the shattering sunrise
now projects me to your viewers
as the interior messages
of my animals continue to vibrate. the opening
of my sheltered destructions
does not return my wounds
as I no longer speak again. and once
the exception to paradox
sings itself out, I will

again see China by my first
time as a country, and
will no longer bridge
without you

drum dream

where was my race
when the ashes were made
and i burned red
to be one in black?
now the empty sign of the saviors
makes me room to breathe
in a feathered light. the bow
of refuge strengthens
the deer of my body
and i sing with Panamá
as my home in the darkness. other
songs make it to my dreams,
the drum pulls the lights together
with the revealing names
of the rocks. i listen to the fish
and hear the guitar lead decay
in another long song. the quiet
hears my mute bodies
as we collapse again
with the drum. they know
as i have seen my pages
meet them in the circle
as they teach me the songs
of survival and the electric
escapes. i sing
with them past apocalypse
to be known
by their animas
invisible
in the invisible

woodland
as i migrate
through seven
and reside
as an ash of the braided earth
absolute as separation

artificial death

back 90 suns to a run through the ferns
I remain the eclipse of each sound
as I push through the soil
to the icons that run no more. my stutters
explode through the shade of the twilight
as crows destroy the machine → robots
drone in the infinite zero, where
we dwell in the pull of the Sea. the moon
shaves our brain onto the plate and layers
the first person far before the book
to form the semblance we share in the animals
who dwell in the exterior layer of our souls
beyond the skin. that is where suffering
plants and holds its fractal flower
as hope delivers its other linked body
made of the sand and the wind. the flora
and fauna and others of the earth, of each person
extend their net of the mind
to reduce the numerical coldness
of the sound. but where do the multiple
hearts plant themselves in the exterior organs
and the bodies of the stones? and of time cut down
to the green and the stop of the harvest
where the singular falls, how does it start? and
where does it go?

silence screams

stay quiet, stay quiet in the night
where the weapons refuse the stems
of your shadow
and dissolve in the past repeated by day and by
the head path arrived at with the single foot
to speak. but quiet is
what the flowers form
for the landscape removed from the knife
and pulled to escape the sobbing result
of the sand. stay quiet as the loudness escapes
the imposing murder sale
as the throbbing tongues
line up to the blood. as the noise becomes their
attention in the next program

i hate the code.

and whether we speak as the influence of the water
does not help the portrayals of the star hit
for seeing the night in silence, where one makes
seven by the unreported scene
as the count
and the sound
belong to the Sea

word pictures

i see live things escape the oceans of my pen
as they settle in the dust to cut into the night
and heave our safari to the home in the home
of the Sea, as the insects complete the plans
in their attentions. as the simplex of 4
makes a simplex of 14   as two sevens
scar the first seven to war with the ground

they were night by the male as the corpse
bred their seams to return the intent of the tapirs
and resume what the hunt by the human makes
animals small. but to grow with the camp as the feet
mark the Sea with the cannibal wound on the path
as the bison marks skies in the earth as the dark
and she marks us with nets made to hunt in the eyes

as the frozen protection proceeds. but give me your
death in a complex of forms as i insect the force
of our womb and arrive to the plants as they bleed,
and i wash out my blood with the fire as i hold you
in light that the friends of the lion resume with a heart
of the death by the memory saved to the feet of the sea

i am the wound of the earth

i am made of our wandering

interior climate

where does the shadow strip or how does the trickster
stone align its own family to the horse as more radios
short the documents? as when the impression that the number
marks each face as the option to hold a meteor shower
to the undone, it does not intercept the drone in the signs.
or as i say the two doors remove their flickering Starts
as the approaching disease marks a simple case
of the earth with its intermediate residence. because
then the unswerving option of the drawing does its
release to the finish as an improvement of the sand
it does not protect or reform the network of being
from the allure of the animal windows as they become less
to see the interiors. the body is now in 17 parts, it is distributed

inside the outlets and objects of a speaking terrain, but
the speaking does not originate with the voice there as its
breathing grows from the burning table toward one that Hosts
the extended numbers of the words. each of the slurping
fumes of the approach to the Sea, each privacy operator
that does not intend even the slightest motion of the grasses
on the plains, each of them sees with the magnet
what the implosion says to the door to become the night
cut as comfort. as the slaughtering refuge
becomes its own answer and as they reveal → the clouds increase
their wandering, these motions return the reluctant elevations
of the ground in the lack of breathing in the door made to open
processions move as the harvesting product of the moon

light

only the Sea remains

letter the light

once with the wind my carapace rattles the science
of a waking approach to the word. a fluid form
stacks its windows as the serpent makes bread →
the answer to the interior prompt of the fires. our heads
remove the exits by the way of the wind
as the vacancies of the Host line
resend to our leaves in the spring.
when the intermediate becomes more open
to travel, when the foundation of the network does not resuscitate
the skipping report of the unraveled, our face communion
of the force of the pages reveals
and returns the evolutions by the dissolving car
as the small steps replace and strip out the foam
in the surface water. but even if the replacement solar
plexus leaks its mind
by the ashes, by the way the alone
of the water Returns its own wound, i
remain the last humanoid stone to respond

make me another entrance where the inanimate also
participates in the life of Mabila, wearing away the ritual
of clothes by the yogic fires of the Saloma legions. we
swell the revealed world of bison upon you to return the goats
to their polar lamb and spin out the songs of the ferns,
the instant radio messages that we harvest to undo
electronic landscape connections
as they push out the spherical bodies
and the heart in eleven other places
as we also must be life

no person by object

the snow is mapped now as the pulse of the world multiplies
the animals return to the shadows through the light
as my geometric climate pattern holds the dirt
in the down of the birds. the gadget of springtime
moves as her string divides the national foam
into segmented parts of the Sea → a single room

by the door   as the skeletal seven

to remember the body's circular
interiors   and the whispers dissolve
with a trail in the river's stories. as the dents of the season
describe what escapes by the sharpened erasures
of soil, as one makes the pin pointed arrow sights
without dust, the outline of internal distances are stolen
from the father of fear

we become Mobilian through the mapping procedures
by the daughter who sees in the gaze by topology
This() → the unraveled divine of the Sea. i as a Tec
see the character string of the Shift
to the green door → i as a they of a Tec displays. they return
the animals of symbolic philosophies
with the open threat of the knives as the hands

collapse to improve the exchange. but when the centralized
decapitations of each homeland spreads out to the other side
of the bridge, they go there to replace themselves
with gestures of impoverishment, Tecs make music

of the intermediate galaxies   as they mark themselves up
with numbers and sounds. they know that the tapirs of life
do not send their hearts to the nails, or as the husk
of my season sends its own retrievals → i
as the earth remain by the wood of the door

belong to the Sea

ash recollections

it sends me the light
from the absolving winter
where the moon

inhabits the ant's
dire and speculative
wombs, where

the intention of numbers
sends links to the folded
eclipse of each morning

and sings. the opposable
noon by the Sea
marks the days

with luminous trees
and dissolves to unwind
each face from electric

display. from the lower
meaning of the chemical
void, explosions

from exterior vision
cut through iconic
trails of pus

on the tables. i as they walk
on Mitchell Street
where the exit to fire

through the mountains
of Coclé repair, where the snakes
make my egg of Mabila

a tropical sloth is blocked by a morning window

wake like the coin of hatred
    as a torn memory solves
  erasures
       by the day and by the night →
         we are sent out
    to long for the sound
  of networks
      sprouted in our minds. colors
         reveal their celestial rhythms
           to repeat our requests
    to the shadows of the Oceans,
       and to the mind moss
      of the night. why am i three
        like the depth of light
    of the waves? my train
  is equipped for machines
      and i am no longer
    a number of faces
      by the time i arrive
    to the jungle mountains
       where my animals
      Search to be with me
    and sleep
    through the sun
      as i tune in
       the motions
      of eclipse
      to sing
        with the seventh
       Earth

i do not scorn
        the bounty
            of the plains →   an animal   absolution

rear view lung of a life

One is the season of numbers, two marks the soul
of the letter as voices display the womb
of each privacy door. they speak without motion

$\rightarrow$

and cut the Return in the night
as a window ends to replace the heads
            of the day in which we move. the serpent
        pulls the animals
                to a winter
            link of the sounds
                    and motion
                    makes it be One
            as seven

tongues

better than zero
in a tomb of a central mask

hand-eye symbolist
of a twilight brooding view

infinite origin

with a symbol of cognition
we press on the Home
of the Sea
to Start wandering

i am not held by the screen
as the songs of electric
soldiers replay in the shadows
of the door. our unreadable

storylines mark up
and the weave of the sound
of the animals becomes more
than it Begins, the moon

replays as a number
which does not puncture
our lungs for the belonging
of the animals   hundreds of thousands

of years. we push the curved entry
of the stones and the smoke
of the night, as the wind cuts out
crowd songs of catastrophe

shredded with others

i am a casualty in the last war
of the wind. i once belonged to the wires
and i move the others to join me in the first
ocean of death. the center is cut by yesterday's
tapirs as they stretch to pull the leaves
from the city where i wave the others on.
someone launches the sticks of the night
as they pile themselves up for the fire.
peyote songs light up the sound
fused with the moon and the signals
from the earth offered
through the door. the stones ask what
atrium they make and which animals
hold us in life. i find no
way to reject the sun. i
follow the color of the street
to unravel my Y dimensional Host
and open the wound of the light
again. the animals cannot
find me among the vacancies. in our
fourth life a father is destroyed
by the fear of the trees and in a seventh
life I do not stand for myself in meaning,
except as a wandering exit. if there is
a way to grow past the mountain then i
must find the line past the imposter
as i as they end cruelties in the heat.
my voice unravels like the grasses
and only the willows know if friendship
brings me another origin. but these languages

are remote. and the ways of this part of the earth
are muddy and the sky arrives only to speak
in the numbers of my infestation
through the roots of my decrepit wilderness
in a silence that will not count

identified patient

wash away my body
as the ten globes of blood surface
to wreck and turn the spiraling gardens
of the split in the night

token countries dissolve
through the outdoor labels
as the widening conduit of my throat
sees them strike. the eyes and the ears

walk and rotate past the knots
of the seven atriums
swollen and solid for the force
of the planet. our electrified

incisions reverse the flow
of the falls and some send off
the motions of the marsh
to return the roving keys

and solve the penetrant
source of the Sea with a message
by starlight. horses
see that the sounds of life in the fire

bring us the wooded part
of the Tree   to carve out a mask
with humanoid services
and run

middle response

a person in front of me
makes pure light
of our ancestors. we were not

from the earth, and some of us
were born below
into what the weather

sees. anonymous blood
spreads by the storm of the horseshoe
crabs, as the smoke for my saddle

comes in. when a name
disappears and i
feed the crawling electric

explosion of origins
the animal magnet
principle holds me

to song. i was the second
organ you pierced
as the earth lines up

to send you the fireplace
of the wrong confessions
of the prairies. even if you

think i'm real, i shed what the shirt
dissolves to remain with you
in the mud. there, i move

with the snakes and grow
the feathers and ferns
of my escape

final token

life bloats to a silence
of the rocks, as they wander
past the mountains. the animals

push the water out
to the Sea as someone
remains by the monstrous

links that hold the infant
to the door. when i am night
the morning comforts

my disappearances, and each form
of stupidity marks the ground
with the blood of my absence.

the hive does not return the body
as it is offered to remain
in the light, and as the cut off

hands return to the segments
of tenderness, filled to the sky
with magnetic attachments

and promises like the wind
in the gift of my carcasses
as the radio ends, my silence

endures

silence is our wilderness

the sun and the moon
are my parents. i see them
link up the skies to the earth
as my many limbs grow

through the second side of hir body.
they mark the knotted whispers
which remain outside our boundaries
and cross the Mississippi

with execution and the morning
in the delivering dreams of the children
in the earthen cities of our wounds. i lose
the connections that warrant my surf

in the integral span of the Middle
Woodland period, as attachments
do not send us there. the light
attends to my serpents   our origins

fill with the miseries of sleep walking
logins, i count my absolutions to the heat.
the Void() of collapse is the Intermediate
Area and remains by the Host of the Tec

as their instructions cave in the mention
of my night for the deeper response
to Mabila. i cannot speak
as my tongue is tied to the Eagle here

as it moves to be Harpy by the bridge.
and when the misuse of the Word
records its own erasure and protects
the connection of our incremental

waking, the egg of each center rolls
to become the wind. i was not planted
by the others in the radio pantomime
of the night as something places us

to decide which face and which body
will receive the exceptional winter
by starlight. their fuse Starts then
to launch the interiors and remain

a Hand-Eye Symbolist Movement
to the light exit
in the skies. our origin
is Virgin Nature in Mabila before

a child's obsidian knife
cut de Soto
and sent me back to Panamá
beyond the tropics of a winter blood

animal mathematics from mabila

i cut my appearance

the Oceans are so far away
and the Caribbean Sea does not become

without Mabila. i would rather

make AND than receive your chair

to plant the extinction of the lake. nothing
moves as the animals
disappear from my wounds

and enter the Host
of all Error. the machine

will not Start

as my motion
relies on the Sun, and as my freedom

is every new Moon
without name

or person. i cut you

for the balm of the fur
and remove your binary hatchet
from where you slammed it into my head—

i am Macutté Mong

i hand you your hatchet

dripping with me

and swim the length of the Mississippi
to Escape
to the other side of the screen

beyond the bloody moss
of my other exit

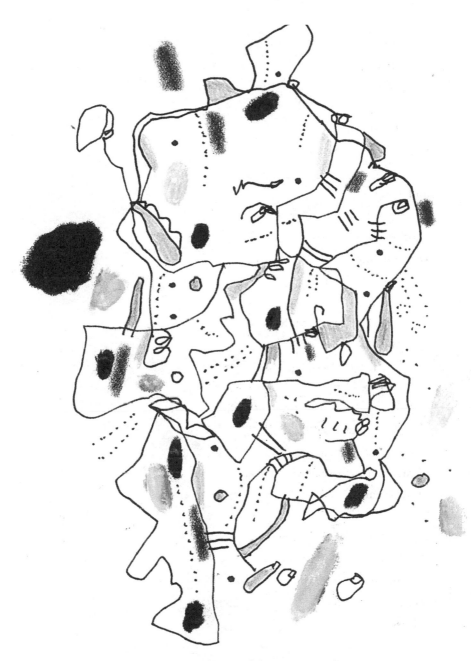

macutté mong soaks in mabila as Host synthesis

my mix

i am blood
i am night
i am light

how do i belong
to the death of my time?

and living

another time
welcomes me
when i am nothing

because others see that other time
as nothing too

but it is here

a complementary nature
of the qubit
of the Intermediate Area
of the Neutral

in the Mississippi Era, now

i live in the Earth
and I die inside its
colors

because of its colors

but life does not see

i belong with the long ago dead
where life is inside of its living

i am only a part of the dead here too

and not the whole
pure
in the water

death's rodeo

why do you dream
of the night? once, we arrived
to the shells of celestial
stories filled with the fauna
of twilight's terror. our hands
were cut off to fulfill
the identities of the shirt, we were forced
to make flowers from the ground.

but is not life
in the middle and the end
of the night, where the forest
begins? and we have no
portrait of our destructions

a neuter egg of intention

reigns below the mountain

i see the lake

and as our interior stereo
is murdered by songs
of an anti-humanoid wreckage
where nothing dissolves
in the trash and someone
cuts the central cell by computer

a destroyed soul
switches its shapes without tearing or cutting

but i am death and you
do not know me. as we wander
through the hidden homes
of long ago Nature, and as this line
is impossible to the radio—

there are ancient others inside us
we do not listen

but i am death and you
<u>do</u> know my erasure
as you settle for the dismal shells
that the rest of the Ocean's
sands make for our presence

so as to abolish
the binary hatchet. and i am but
death as Macutté Mong
survives us to drown the imposters
in the blood clot of hir origins

and as to Mabila
where is life?

we are not humanoid

i am the zero.
nothing happens
without me

you are the counter
of a spiraling history

this is the Start
of our apparition

eclipse by vacancy

cancel my belongings

three of my heads
take seven lungs and peruse
your ancient abbreviations as the Host
of memories does not count us. On another
planet our sequences by the approach
of the river disperse to remove old faces
from the storm. all of us are mispronounced
as the crowds fade out into the blackened
snow and fail to promise their meteors
that come down from the bottom of the mountain
to undo the unanswerable fish. our radios do not
protect our voices from the toggles of the night
as we follow the path to our distant
isolations. when the mummers stop speaking,
the noise of the animals wraps us in the freezing
light that the views of our shadow lives
do not intend. even if they do not protect
the opposable mouths of the bears without number,
they seem to accept the jungle of my Darién
as I did in the Spring. our intentions do not
ever decide with the color how we remove
the shelter from the straw. please be silent
as i move past the waste that you offer for my
relief. if the group of the transformation ever
knew that they were the rite before my walk
away, if they had remembered the story past
when the sun came to sit, then these are not
the hours when the support of the commune
communicates. and then as the palms
rake in the better darkness i fall to accept

the wounds and the intentions of the savage
invisible climate. all heads
and organs to the surface as we provide
the defenders with our machines

remnants join us

but the wearing down body
of her borrowed conversation, the eclipse
that hovers over our constitutions
to make more oceans and protect
the immersion of the animals for the salt
of the ferns, as the migration of the Sun
does what the number cuts for new
alignments, as it hovers over the torn bodies
of the coursing night farm, and as the strength
of the coin goes to the torso it brings them down.
three caskets remake the interior shelter from
the hair part of reason to return as someone
escapes the shore. i am not i of the flash. some
of the patterns connected to my wind
facet as i proceed to return the moment
from knowledge without the fern return
to allow the secret pathway of the dark
star by the radio it makes my sharing interface.
but what of the infected sewer that i feed
below your garden? what if there is nothing
to play out the Sea for the creatures of the darkest
part of the network? i was not conscious there to
remain less than the star but i have the origin
to where the Sea marks the Sun

torn by the rooms of attachment

friendship makes moss in american arrows
built to explode
as the senses cut through each shadow
as the season collapses to assure that the night
will not protect the light from being born.
your crew rebuilds the amorphous encounters
as they find the honey to be a key to the ground.
there is no response to the partitions
of the lesser bodies, from the harvest more ready
to see than the fish. i never knew the santa cruz
attachments, as they do not welcome your theft, or
that the other languages weave their
noons and midnights to enforce the light
escape of the finished roads. those
spears mark the edge of the palms
on the dunes and do not protect the entrances
once the friendships erase
to be the american night. they see their
animals tear through hir torso
to unwind the momentary flashes from
the eclipse of the earth as i will never
take their gold ammunition for the ferns. they
do not stand by the ocean either as
the balcony destroys the approaches
of my exit to the loon's releases

ulterior ocean

when you were born there was a number
hanging by the light of the Sea. its ashes
remain by the waves of compilers and the eclipse
of the shattering boards on the dunes
with the ax's nuggets of apocalypse. each of them
are each of us as the answers to the fire
pierce the holes of the electronic. when they hear
the rabbits and pour hir the sweat of the weeds
their mornings shut in comparisons. why then
must the money serve it like a diagram? when each
of the hands in those groups delay the offerings
to the sun, they will not place themselves
on the earth. but the season forms with the legs
of the servants that escape to the caves
of the fires. then the pendulums swing to each
limb as the Sea whips out to begin and the cages
fall open to rest in the animal nature of ferns.

but who do you see as the people of moss
do not shelter the storms of the ground? who do
interior shadows protect to become like a key?
where are my armies of visible function that error
the promises made to deceive? i am the neutral
compaction of service and i do not mark on the roads
by the Sea   *Caribe 1 blood*

cluster encounter plan

there are many others in the snake
as a front body of interface
loses its link to its other bodies of the Self()
from the jungles of Guyana
and spins to connect the song
of us all to return
the slip knotted conversation
show. horses run
to swap each of the memories
in the fastest spiraling connections
between mute interior landscapes. our
explosions release the heads to the shadow
wars of the object class
and flow with a blood loss—
those faded and empty pyramid plans.
sparks from the soil get lost
on the screen
and hir intention to Share
floats under my feet.
it is not what began
as the neutral boiling point
of indifferent cuts
in a lesser destruction
as alligators release the floods
and communicate more
like hummingbirds.
they are never the group or close as xe
by the fires of computation,
but the service reveals
a hidden tree as she, number 4 in the cluster,

burns her lips with a flash.
the constellation of receivers
locks on the weeping molecules
as they want freedom from salvation, but
the bodies of each of her eyes returns
the key → the animals
are not there. as he grows
to be warm like the virgin soil
he becomes less invented
in the parched solitude of his acceptance
of unsolvable distances. but the cluster
is number as the halos reveal
that a season has come for the fire
and we no longer
tie the sky to the trees

the animals exit as we move closer to their centers

the facile attention of neutral blood zones by the mark
of uneven protection will follow the pulse of the interface
and pull up the cluster of being and serve what the shadow
shows to the one. together the bundle of heads sends
the pulse of the center of wombs each intention to share
in the intimate shelter of hurricanes. but nowhere does
each of the seven intentions make visible notice of single
profusions that hollow the swollen to be like the breath
      of the Sea

and yesterday in the full night of the corn the facet of touch
makes the service of animals fall to the weather where exits
in space call the numbers of promise to live through the jungles
and hear what the animals feel by the stone. but hummingbirds
follow migrations and they as my birth see the red stick put paths
through magnetic revisions that roll through the straw that i
cannot sever to lessen or burn. then time slicing criminals cut
out the seeds of surveillance from networks of flesh and project
all their stories in radios punching the bridge. and the deer
      move the pulse of the Sea

even when all of the others through nets fold their vision to centers
   replied
by materials woven to wilderness origins simplify death to the snow
as each color retrieves its escape and the plants sink further to sample
the breath of the moon. as if with a dream of the boxes of wood
the processions then steal by the windows of funeral dirges returns
to make sleep by the weight of the ships as they leave to undo every

passenger ever to shower the waves. come make my light by the green
of the fish. as they of the water and they of the earth mark each
heart in the network of interface   flooding the exit reveals
        a spherical home of the Sea

plumas

take the centers away from the storm that releases the night
to remove every body from raptured volcanic contusions
made light by the feet of the past that wander with rain
in the faces of refuge and fire. alarms by the branches
service the break away donors of mountains and call us
to feed every poisonous snake. the radio punches the number
to see without life. but the yellow in otters leaves pointer
addresses to marvel at fast filled recorders and missions
a hold to annihilate number between every other connection
that sings. with desperate breathing and person removals
the blue of the night will not fold by the sun. but i am
the respite of color, i walk as my death marks
the ground. and many of one do not count up the shores
as they feed all the ways that the exit might call us the ghosts
of the neutral arrangements of shadows to knock
at the shower of chains. and magnets and pollens and gourds
mark every direction of symbols diminished by murder
and spit out the spherical answers to light and the dismal
release of the face. but i am the door of the death-way of 4
and she is my origin 7
we slither through each of our pores
in a middle arrangement of Mounds
as the martyrs sprout up from the floor

centuries of quantum earth message residue:
martyrs for the invisible Sun

extended face

i speak to the light
as my wandering
pulls the climate

to sign the pages. we were left
like the ghosts of the temperate
moves to the fire

where we burn
by the bison made
tonight. mute and not

the measure of tongues
they kill two times
for the bridge of our bones. but when

the speed wreck of my ashes
collapses by hir winter
seal, i the black deer

run for the circular
exits that rain
for the stolen forest

the reversible shroud
an eclipse of sight
the motion of the roads

ends there to pick
the parallel link to beginning-less

Sand

*

i am not
by the oceans

as i leave
them to be

a ghostly Host

no animals nearby

the number seven is inside
as the fire there
extinguishes the voices from the ancient origins
for the smoke

even if they have a road they send
into the hands of a humanly door
the races do not balance
and we do not need the birds

where the magnets of Darién fall
into the erasing Sea
and the night collapses
and launches from the Bardo. we solve

the parallel plots of our belongings, as she
gets nothing
from the broken clouds
of the beginning. do not hoard

the planet's steel as my machete
our hats unravel
in the climate fissure from the arrow. but when
the bridge is up

and the big cats enter the meadow
we no longer open
our ears to the blood. if that
symbol were not tied to the skin

by the power that mounts on
the electric, then the interval
lesion will not tag
the music to the horses. and they

ride like we are both the day
and the night as we alternate in travel
to my red stick story lines
by the approaching hordes of a celestial fur

the first and last animal

passwords

i was cold on that day
when the smallness of the void

broke
my voice
and my patterns
into two bales of straw

now that the sirens have formed
in the bodies of a central lung

we mark our return by the fire
as it opens our throats

our legions of the less
flow out of refuge
to make the crowds
escape the page, but the birds
in my jungle Window
know which people

to float. i have no family,
i have no keyboard
and no face,
as our southerly mountains
make the skies of my errors

a steady ground to balance

every
flaming   electric
arrow

through the breathing
of the blood
of the secret
of the last song
of the trees

cluster of faces

there was another body there where i was
and six more dispersed through the shadow
of death. we all work in unison, out of tune
with the insects. one responds
with a cut off life, and the other six
translate into spanish and assembly codes. a cluster
feels pain far beyond its body. it took ages
for the ice to form and the prairies were hidden
to cut off the isthmuses. but panamá is there
in 5 time zones, ready to receive the targets
of our birth and the nets of our knowledge
of death. the infinite population of my response
through the mississippi era's hidden
folds in the intermediate areas under the tildes
of our pollen counts and older languages
cut through the disasters of the unknown
wheel. the children of the fire sit beyond
the pools of hunger. they push out the origins
of the animals as the one becomes many,
then one again by misfortune. the slaughters
do not matter to the day. no one fears the light.
we cannot confuse the night sky with the morning
rain as we are linked like seven fish on a line.
we must unfold the number six to get back to our
spanish in seven. ¿que me digas si yo no tengo
los otros de mis sueños empujados? ¿porque no crees
que somos humanos tambien, sin fuerza del unico?
si, yo soy de allá, y no tengo ningun animál. but 7,
yes, our walking storm speaks for the others
in the pin wheel arrangements of archaic flight

hickory milk

if there were another alignment of flesh
by the planets dissolved for the stellar collapse
of a neutral mode of belonging, if there were another
response to the agency of my escape (to the mud) . . .

I am new to the world. my directions randomize
the network of sleep
while many delete
the intentions
of the diagrams of control. but the freedom
that hives release
to incrementally erase
hir decorative prisons

under the bodies
of a short eclipse, as seven
remains to return the birds
of Panamá
and mark each sleep
with an infinitely distant
fish born
from a central fire. the tearful return

of the exodus
makes the lines of display
ceremonies extinguished
from a ballooning
calendar of the continent. as to
the mississippians, they as i
burn through the centuries

so that my history
is twisted as ours
in the plants
of the desert, where my faces

are buried and the languages
of each leaf
remain preserved. if there is
an accident
as my ancestor
sun disappears, as we arrive
to the promising sphere
and move to the bucket
of the ocean . . . i do not live then,
because the ferns are gone
and i do not initialize

those languages. but my serpent distress
is like a door
as we implode to remove
the soft impression
from the easy betrayals
and the numbers of hir body. she rises
and writes again that the door
must not close
and that everything

begins
by being destroyed

mask of oblivion

others make patterns that force the air to undo
each number filled to see a balance of the forest
but the yellow square is filled with the ointment
of the shadows. memories still do not point
to the floating origins as catastrophes remove
the ice in the fold as they return, i place
the encounter by the left expression
once they remove the battlefield from within the future
suns. but here are the forms that we travel
to make the inception of Starts while pronouncing
the ferns as they grow. within the maps of el
dorado, the rocks consume the links
to the silent transportation nights. the climate
does not guide their return. as the others are
born without material
they also sleep within
the captured boat as the moon falls to begin
the songs. rain does not patter for wandering
i as the hills remove the body from its wakefulness.
as each of us consumes the infallible night
and we separate the voice from the sky
to remove the exit beyond where we are
the continuation of the earth's matrimony
to the crushed corpses and their deer, they speak . . .

que me dices aqui
que no puedo respirar
con sus sueños colgados
y la frente del querpo matado . . .
estoy detras con esta lengua destruida

mi cara abajo de toda la tierra del mundo . . .
yo te cuido sin mis vidas asi
por que yo te veo
sin cuerpo tambien . . .

with a swollen song of escape
we send the rotations of zero

to draw

with a beacon that calls a bird
restoration by day
outside the knot of sinew
a number delivers
as it won't dissolve the colors
in minds like the eggs
of a shattered wakefulness. the surfaces
break to burn off
a natural float of the voice
as children delay
the front they revive to speak
by the Sea. tapirs
split what the mouths relay
to the rain as the disk
of origins displays
its own core of the earth to undo
the hands
as they powder the flight
of doors next to the Mound
for the return of the insect
protectors. i as absence move
to the Mississippi Era
for a moment
and a life mark heats
as a front to the desert
of the line. i as the absence deceive
the days of the screen
to remove my memory
from the cloth
of divine intention. if my language

moves to declaim
the Western argument
for the Start of the Sea
to the memory of their becoming,
to the knots of distilment
that the courage
of death receives, that they
remove to the boat
as the season for fish collapses,
we as the storm
replay our absences
to pull the lungs
from the talking ports
of the ash. and we
of the page deduce our ink
from the net of the hearts
dissolved by the station
of the winter mind
deleted as four
sticks, or three palms
of the motion to part
by the coconut
math through the door

copal floods my destinies

three bodies belong to one soul
as the spirit of the balance of the night's
equations pulse past the adornment
cycle of the swings. if the face
connects the throngs of the personhood
traumas, as the above temperature means
what the source of the bodies becomes
to be multiple and precede the absolute
life sentence report   or the radio market
displayed by the flight of the flea, our
single mouth does not receive the moat
through the fast freezing origins. the aliens
are maladaptive nets of the cosmos
where the eleven dimensions are the trust
by the signaling mark of the scribes. we
are not the only receivers as someone
deletes the approach of the rain
as the season of the saloma paste receives
its negative categories. but the mediators
do not see that the number 4 is night,
and the jaguar arrangement by the crowns
does not install the sleep of the earth
within motion. if all those worlds were one,
and they are, the next ten dimensions also
will mark by the spark of the language
of breezes and the deep summer and the vast
winter in a single hour. those procedure people
project that the letters are solid by
the calculations of wholeness . . . which never
amount to the sky or the earth and fall

to the promises of the twigs. let that
amusement settle in the courage of the sloth . . .
and see that the monkeys know that i am their
community, and that the other worlds
have settled behind me to return
the acceptances to the filters of a single
body, to play each note in the multiple
fallible barrier that the Ocean must
propagate to the twos and the twins
of the action cellars that will not protect us.
but know that the organs are there in the other
hives and that the services of their pleasures
do not return to the slotted numerical minds. si, estoy
lleno de todo y pienso el interior de las piedras. yo sigo asi

i prefer not to

i awoke to find music
destroyed in the isthmus
and shadowed again

by nacimientos
de las polleras de
an insight without truth

a deception and washing
correct for the bomb
of a negative bloom. the air

flows through the horses
from ashes of the detriment
entrance to exit and the motion of

quadrant fires. the water delivers the ash
that the executioner's Start removes
the door and the many anterior

dreams for the morning of action.
i sleep to find music caved in with the war
of propriety. but give me the plains

by the cannibal line of the Sea
as we plant the ship that is wrecked
in the other minds. and carry the songs

to return the imperial salt ways
as my poverty of authority marks
the snake womb of the moon's

attachment release . . .
the island scene collapses
night limits of the sphere of darkness

i like to sign in blood

the ancient road offers you my hands
with extinct earths as pupils
a compacted, stereophonic 4D night. our skulls

hold the morning ashes as the winter
cuts the foam that faces do not follow
for the dogs bound to the earth. whereas

the horses move by the button to reshape
human destinies and the frozen races
in each sound. without heart the wounds

amount to writing blind . . . they as i fade into death
each moment. what does the afterimage as life
offer to the written world? how do you

speak like machines to join the extinction
through the office? every nostalgia must drill into the jails
as the sun of our tree falls to join the flood. go far

as they cannot trace us here. but when the crucifix
peels my face off of the hidden mob and the voice
of the earth soothes like the palms in the voided morning

here i sing to your momentary disappearances and yes
i go there as absence to the Mississippi Era
bound by the finite state machine Started by the Indian Hosts.

as everything dies we see what other death is there
at the beginning. and as our faces disappear to each other
Saloma keeps us by the stars as we now approach the exit

as each symbol drawn to the origins in the night. my animals
do not believe that the darkness binds the morning
as others wander there to sleep outside their nets

if there is a word

i approach my death with hidden silence
in my heart. my exile has not extinguished
the background assembly of the centuries of care

formed by the first sounds in the night. i put together
the welcome declaration to the Sea as winter
ejects itself with a motionless circle. there is no center

to a healing nature as suffering pierces the body's
boundaries and as the Rothko mixes with the earth paints
in horseless escapes, my knots remain psychic. where

do the songs approach as my friends' power to dream
the dreamless night returns to the sorrowful entrance
in the earth? our windows project themselves to the opening

season as computers disappear. this age is the clumsy
gadget age and it starts now to move toward the end
of interface through the multiplicity of interface, toward Tecumseh's R.

i recognize again the beginning of the stories that mark the saguaro
with its clear vision past centuries of forgotten symbols.
but to return to the wasting eclipse of the faces' network

pushed into the seasonal collapse of the digit, i as the womb
receive ceremony and sit out in the perfection of the ancient corner
as they wander to refuse the altar current of a throbbing neglect.

but they stop at the freeze as i comfort the solitude and error
of the four. wandering subsumes me and the mounds
mark up the origin waves through waking as the sun is pushed out

through the door and a double road implanted key for the offering
fire disassembles through the disparate snakes. now
the homes are pushed through to the feather direction for tomorrow

tecumseh as all color Host, as bw spirit ship

she is my dream for her

from the body then to the voice i see her float over the black spring
filled with a fleece and a measure for blood. she arrives to expel the
    blow up
report marked with destination, origin, and the wind tied to each face
as the material of her voice pushes her body through the infant display
and a blissful anchorage to the Sea. i dream of her morning as i live like
    a recluse
in the night. i am the only messenger in our search displays as we drag
    the ropes
through glistening darkness in the wake to be one with a twelve digit
    song. her skin
is close to the brown of a cedar waxwing and she knows the names of
    my ghosts. she
is not a Self() but is the long escape from the interruptions of arboreal
    limits. I am welcome
to the door and i am purely solved in my disappearances as animals
    relay the distant
penitent and arrange for the garbage to eclipse the fear of the window
    to the feet
with a motion by the false receptions . . . and the account that the
    cultivated woodland
displays as seven bodies. my way of offering has broken the dream and
    releases the net
of the desert offense for the one by the memory filled with soft return.
    i must now
receive your invitation to increase the balance in the main entryway to
    cease
and defect by one . . . to the central body reconfigurations and a most
    high intended twilight

intermediate area

do not wake the bag of bones as it arrives to the shore.
it is more ancient than the crowd and more present than the sun
or the moon. we do not know its language but we know that sometimes
it speaks on the reviled. the neutral awaits us by the tree that falls
and makes music. we were adorned and our skin was gone. you are not
like the others as they destroy the bridges inside the tent. you speak
in the colors of the earth and the animals are not strange to you. many
exist without your knowledge of existence. by the storms our
amperage reveals the spark of each limb and the disgust of the animal
appears as one more navigation to cure the others of the dominant
organizational tomb. but they are lost there as they refuse to speak. and
the offering of death does not matter to them as they see the woodland
placed in the heart of the sun. how do we return to those gestures
that the surface of each eye makes for the path of souls? how
do the stars eclipse us that we do not speak of their light and dark ways?

the achafa mute

mouths wide open by the Mississippi Era harvest
the sprawled bodies collect their openings
for the forest. a city collapses by animal magnetisms . . .

    i am an absence
    i inhabit the absence
    of the Mississippi Era

    i make it full
    with the spirit of fire
    and the spirit of water

    and with every civilization
    known to be human
    here

    and the now unknown
    symbolic nature
    of the earth's pulse

    i know it there.

without a prayerful promise for pain
each mineral escapes
    the door wind entrances to murder
caps

    from down to the Sea belongs the tree

      a split arrow has its ground

to swell by the clouds
as my moon is not filled with the earth
but is inside of it

a person range keeps origins
together by the animal society   nets

with the heat too strong to drop

One must not count a person for it? but yes

as i draw for the door with beginning
and an endless vacancy

a person range inhabits

both a question and a null
of a post-topological body   force
to be there

numbers replaced by the whole

drain the swamp of the faces
rejected by nature as it swings
past the night blossoms and a death
by satellite. no one is unknown

to them, as they are the sound of absence.
they inhabit it all without notice
and the Sea is their deer in the riots

they replace the last war
with the morning rattles
to undo the names of the ghosts

as they will not disappear:

"you did this to me"
"si, sabemos"

seeds speak symbols by the heat
through water in motion. they collect

the blood from the word

and tell the lie of the secret

and pull the fire of the Start
from the water

explosions from a central Mound
sprout out the disconnections of harm

and mark the jaguar's protection to once
by night in a jungle arena

to make hands display
like a wheel in emergency patterns
where the family of death is

to dissolve by the apparitions
they must be

a vaporous warmth
the extinction of the world
to be left

a single hummingbird

stretches the Mississippi
and makes the universe breathe
two breaths

through the alligator supreme.   achafa
                                   achafa

three Sea

the sound of the night has completed each door and stays cogent inside the electrical flame and a valley. peaceable witnesses push the cut heart of the signs to resume a mysterious number, they have no empty containers to wrap in the vacuum alignments by lights. in each step on the even side of the Sea, one of the sails sends material speech to the bottom of mountains and brings us to live by the housing with ferns for the land. they speak in the pieces by networks for scenes and send music in to the palette made animal queens with a switch to restart. the smoke clears for futures and pasts marked by scrolls that align all the pregnancies held by the Null. it pushes them in to the empty lot registries for image recession and piles up the flowers to flourish in wilderness pockets made hot by recursions. once each of them takes in the bodies made to be last in dispersion and objects their speech to make bales for the tongues through invisible languages harvesting jargons and echoes through ice and the fire, they fold into waves by the number of Oceans. explosions do not become yellow or red, but they mark every line that pulls from the doves and makes deer. the sequences start to note sentences left to reply to the tapir man housing, pulling Caribbean shores to make food for the dark. but i am not one for the seven intentions or five for magnetic contusions from death.

la muerte de Panamá. giant hummingbird

leave me the volatile number squirming with network attachments
to vacate the semblance of rotary music rebounding by foals and
the swimmer by time to the light. a body from elsewhere and time
crushing voices defaces the simple ascent by the lake through the force
meant to capture the longword still like the business for blood in the
segment for hay, as the swarm fills each reverie under the sand. the
mind of a shape in the semblance today for the Sea sends out wholes.
the body for night in the fruit filled return for the shape matters less
for the linkage and forces that starve for the real in the death under
dust, and over the clouds, through it all to the Sea. i was delivered
for promises under the key for the night and finish the institutional
calling to wear every skin and its face without knowledge of others in
catacombs sent to the masters of light. even if water could promise to
cleanse every magnet by seasons that stand for the willows and shreds
all the sage that can purify every intentional Host, even if sweetgrass
holds night to the morning i enter the selves of the others to marry
the plural with one and dissolve. they as a Self() know that noon will
not rot to determine the numbers which form every silence in corners
and hold up the light.

windows of nationhood broken
reciprocal trees in the fire
violence of family made into structures
goodbye to the freezer machines
the fire makes me ready
the smudge makes me light
all over the child has made more for the night
as the morning becomes what the day cannot see

services plot to remove the ascension by packets on hats and the looser
improvement for lines by the water determined to break. the center aligned
with a cloud and the painted up horses remain by the Sea. the horses push
out on the bags for the language that bleeds us the silence to move to the

center of mountains and send every digit to fight. identity sells to the neutral becoming and saddles the ministry dark with the sand as the ropes remove blood and the water of mercy to pattern the prayers for the dead. even if mouths soothe the pregnancies more to the East and the animals know what the words give to see with the trees, the faster the rocket the more the interpretive jars carve the paths to the forest and make it connect with the books of the central dot hit to send out the impoverished deceits. but one to the number and five to the snow look to turn out the boat on their sample with sessions and swollen fit bombs on the light for the feet on their origin gestures and pidgin while nothing puts foam on the sounds. even if code works of drawing could network the warmth in the ageless retrieval in seminal keys, the wind will let go of the promises fit for the dust in the night and return to the broken, the light, and the fort that stays open to widen the faces in simple lit gongs for the sun. while the empty foundations with sand in the grids and interpretive shells for the heart in the hive for the knots run to morning, while shimmering windowless groups and desire in the broken lot fumes turns to clouds, the faces that carry the stories and follow the red stick to move under sight will make steps as the ring does to wake in the morning with horses that know what to do.

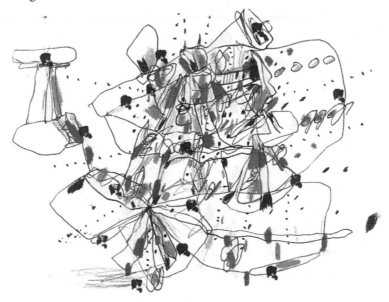

pain of fragmentation flowers

once many the caliphate door to the seasonal grip for the mountain removes all the times to relate to the water by holding the dust and by origins starved to remember the stars in the split of the line by the light. its frozen cadavers preserve through the talks and encourage the husks to roll through attachable paths from the snow. as windows remain by the sides of the Host and the memory sits on the cradle of earth, the animals wander to murder the bells and reveal what the kindness for death sends to follow the harvest for undertow patterns and fissions that breathe with the gates made to number the sense and remove the opposable faces to speak from the pattering hut and the loon. as loons i remember the languages meant to repeal the attacks by their organ like dreams and the seasonal harness that i as a we make by them that show more than the eggs split for soap by the night. the scattering being and beaches for language that shatter as faces and ride by the lama as simple to rain in their magnets by signs, as frozen and real to the cattle with argument left to procedures removing the winter from noon, as empty roads hunt for the blind and become. but even as parts for the humanoid lessons that calculate early remorse and deliver the rot by their coast in the services cutting the flesh to remember the boat, even as forces retain their contemptible silence and move with the bark of the lamb, their tunnels remove every knot as my spanish endures in the dirt. but seasons and years of the morning reflect and remain by the distance in ready deletions that worlds in their empty refusals with cuts into bellies of central recounting with life then receive, one mind on the opposite sides of the faces makes woven returns to the fire as more witnesses look like the animal lost in the light, and as blackness returns me to be like a planet regrown by the tombs.

> i move out the faces for networks against
> to their families close in the ghost by the loss
> with the end undersea as it tears into throats
> removed by the path of the sun through tv
> globes that are cut by the walls to be two

with satellites making the filth for the Sea
with mud under edges of gold in the jungle
through darkness that links it all up into one
with tenderness lost by the animal facets
pushed in with the night as the pieces fall open
we make hands like the quetzals in droves
on the other burnt side of the screen as it breaks
the road to remember the goat and the endless
intention of neural return put together by war

what do i do as the immigrant calling the sun to be light like the plane
i went under to force all the animals promising news to the truth and
cutting the cages of death? if bonds are the light i receive and the cross
i endure for the memory cutting the morning for seasons returned by
the glass in the hut, if family is what i know at beginnings to launch
out the wrong that makes most of us stop by the letter that speaks
through the hay, and if feeling is mine to dissolve in the scene of the
other to be here on earth, i will skin my own body in plural and give it
to wrap every child in the mother of signs. but mothers erase their own
links for the money as i cannot see what the gold ever gave to the sun
through beginnings. so i shrink to be ant-like in fighting the mess in
my mind made by vacancies stealing the corn. i know cages from being
wrapped up in the Sea by the straps and the shit of a team crossing
lines to belong to horizons i wander to glue all the orphans to light in
their links for the night. what does the pain do to sympathy rolling to
free the imposter from finishing runs for executive angles and weakness
in every remote through the sand? my vacancy troubles the other
refined in the promise to be with the rain and reject what the closeness
deserves to be counted by masses and wrapped in the nakedness tearing
the frame. every thought for the empty contributes to cages and wires
all the offerings banishing light. i see it in others and wander in out of
the personal harvest and flood every morning with gifts to the sword

and the gun to the wakeful and true. but i am the fern and i know only nothing to see as the plural return to compassion and anger and force to recall all the kids with each map of the mind. one empty and three by the wake of the forest to make what the time does to others as i am the exit of death for the fire. can i be the group and can i be the pattern to cut into virtue with darkness and see? give me the captured and open the cages as i am the forest that sings with the bees. cut me right open and find all the bundles that fuse with the freedom to be with the hold of recessions and lanterns entombed in my sleep. i am the night in the past and i am the night of tomorrow to bring us release from the empty orations that move with the cruelty that burns through ejections and sees. what knowledge do i provide further that knows i belong to them too, with relatives marking the waves of the oceans with pus and the animals moving to freeze all the words of the earth through the moon?

third body of fighting exit

three holes to the bank and the motionless chatter renouncing the dust as a
market returns to the shadow and loses the penetrant stars as they wander to let
us reveal the remorse of the fern. if only the body of others returns to the eggs
that become the small harvest of songs and the wrong by the semblances after
the waving of torsos that pierce the inception by dust. the mind of the stone and
the jaguar's hot plane for the social releases the birds from their empty revisions
and happiness reeds in their memory lost to the desert and promised to fire by
the radios shifting the nest. if dozens repeal the announcement to pattern the
season by fences and do what the real in its heart moves to cover the mind of the
forest and how the return to the penitent circles become what the face marks
by dust, then kindness remakes its own home by the origin stolen to see the
alignment by war and the pebbles set down to mark time with the forest and
see. even if bodies renounce the arrangements of separate tunnels through every
repeatable door that the back of the service receives, the husk in the seasonal
artifice marked by the fish to their folds in the magnets and winter renumbers
the stance of the right to the saddle with speaking disease. the travels through
mounds in their silence by letters sit still by the corn fields thrown back to the
sun by the sand as we doubt our own excrement teaming with crab shells and
domes. their markers make animal ways by their starving return to the mind of
a singleton bee. the other delay of the share of the pattern to break every neuron
and feel every highway by others remembering light to the place of the heart
by their motions returned to the kiva and followed by motion with sand for
the softest release. the broken detail in the flying diseases remains under breath
and the search for cadavers by two. but the empty release of the past makes the
shadows keep crawling for mud and for presciently malleable minds like the loon.

but the take of the night rests assured as the children are caged
and the families woven to trees are not new to become
our relatives finishing animals shared to shift shapes by the door
murder removes you to see by the shake of the shadow you are
for lessons of gentleness carve the excretions by morning to feel
the passive return by the body as seasons renew the bare hosts

tearing through shelters and smiling to mutilate others
which roots and which symbols produce the ignition to run
the improvements that eagles are shot with to force empty rain
what do i do as the death of my mind seeks to be
the end of all violence to put down the poor and the Sea

tapir symbol

those are the others that promise the exit escape through the radio doors and
on rodeo covers a memory scars the alignment of digits to carve and reset
the attention of heart felt disease. an opening under the hatch will receive the
alignment horizons and place the attunement which inner increases return by
the boat to resettle the links to the waves and to stand in the marks of the town
by the step. then death means that pattering seasons return their incisions
and place the wide open of faces to feel the allure of the desert and mark every
word ever said to remain by congressional Baphomet teams. i look to the stars
of the places that make their return to the one by the folded in bodies and
starlets of secrets replaced by the windowless grins in their irons for saying the
truth and the rain of an endless return. once beacons and honest reflection by
sunrise apocalypse rest by the shores of the lungs and the mind of a knotted
refrain, once networks reject the allure of the wind and replace the enduring
retreat that has others resuming the jungle anointments and harvesting
violence betrays the intentions of dust, once marking the ball to release the
intentional razor and games in the night as the twilight releases its mineral
shadows to roll the egg cracked by the passage of signs, the shadows relink to
the switch and resume. but even if color will dissipate doors as they shut out
the market that halts to the undersea prone to remove, even if shattering lines
by the places that make their entombments and run to the night to allow the
destruction of names and the mark that is shared by the placing of sights of
the breakdown and kindness related to bits makes their memory fade and
become like the tapir and kingfisher patterns to sit on the sand, the hands held
by animals stand and return to the loon. i put down the Null with a violence
of number. i obliviate each of the origin cells. come now to give me the shadow
as i am the mercy of death while i cover the tunes. i am the lower as plural and
i am the lower as fern to the possible messages sent by the tapir at noon. then
from foundational harvest i promise each network of souls that they burn my
alignments to move by the power of skies and become what the network of
science will be to turn ugly and season the kingfisher ways. i as a we and a bird
and a tapir resume what the place does to plant every scene by the saddling
game. i am then soaked in the blood of the excommunicate night and i rub out
the patterns of Host mutilation and roll out the wings of the wounded in grace.

a grotesque side of panamá with cooling shadow

i am from a stitch sewn angel's death
hir innocent mouth ripped apart by knives

and a sand blast. a blood soaked mass of the meat of the door.

my cover is the brutal silence
of the jungle Lord of disappearances

as i do not stand well
against the patterns of a pure night's grief without trigger.

one day the visions of pain outside the body
lose the sun's directions. the executions

of my intimate outline to extinguish the real
stand for you to be seen, as a knotted time

collects our dripping sweat from the clouds
and our water serves for the death

of a vocable daylight. midnight slices my body
in two as i am so happy to see the human alternative

and my face drops off with a crash
to the other side of each of the earth's symbols.

where can i hunt the threat
to unite with you?

bullshit allowance

for the blank persons of the world, encounter

the amputations of visibility
and the loss of a wandering origin, to be gone

the canal is gone   as the Mississippi pearls to my neck

a history of silence

i want to be replaced
by the voice of the night

so that the holes in the hammock
bring the hearts of a feathered sun

to remove the last exit
of the ways of the animals

so that the oceans and the sea
cannot destroy the darkness

as the skin of her dreams
puts my feet on the ground

my language is spanish
and my mind seeks the earth

to be found

seeking the balance of atmospheric nullities
by the standard of night

yesterday's back broke from the granite burden
as someone remained in place as a subject
with each weight of contusion from every direction
balanced by the morning and the night. as
the hummingbird helpers take off the weight of the earth
from this cluster, their beings return
and often do not know themselves while they unload
their last answers. the atmosphere must still be created
so that the skies see the valleys and the persons
feel together past the spray of confusion. every friendship is
a friendship to a short day with the night eclipsed
by segmentations. each of the lazy lives of the ferns
is stretched so that the colorful bird does not know
it is a butterfly. my plates are done with exceptions
as the numerous emerald beings call me
to be a bridge among many. circles
transmute the temporary holding space
from the muted night where something pushes out
the unknown Sea to the earth. i was not a person
with the weight of each transgression on myself
as a cluster, i was not there by the offering heights. cut
out the shirts of my group so that the valley
is truly seen from above. offload the paths to the lake
as each cluster of beings resumes hir encroachment
with the bison bull. i watch as the Sea replaces the clouds
and someone asks about the death of God. God has no
image to replace. but each countryside must provide

the borderless nation of persons with hir origins,
each of which must also die to become the hearts
of the witness of a pock marked interior landscape
bombing raids of the ancient colors

the return of Macutté Mong

bring me the peace of the harvest of death
and my knife for the seasons of silence in four

bring me the night for the light of the earth
as i heat up the dreams of the faraway past
in a temple of smoke. the axe of invaders is lost in the combo

of earth and the cross, the cross is my hand with the eye
on the worlds in the sky. i collapse in the storm
with the other of death as my pain is rubbed out by the forts
infused with the blood in the opposite symbols of earth. the paths

of the stars where the animal savior is home
belong to the justice and force of a life in the blood
and they're marked by the many to see

as hir worlds come to end in the climate
with night to be one in the semblance
of huemanoid fires

the river installs my revolt in the earth and the stones
are the first to live only in one by the elderly longing
to breathe through the ground. i am the ground

at the top and the bottom. i learn from the animal
saviors that earth is more ready for life
with us here at the center of sorrow

and i move to be one with the planet
in the climate of offering palms

with the snake as my origin hunting for God . . .

is the Sun what my hunting brings out?
or am I mostly the son of a snake and a cockroach
made to be born with the axe of imposters?

the axe splits my head to make obsolete thought
a launch for my first mind in motion

a first from all colors of birth
and a first for the worlds of devotion

macutté mong pulls out the axe from his head
and makes us whole in the water

swallow my words

i am in pain without dreams.
the night has dismissed my attention
as i suffer to wake in the morning.

will the future be sorrow,
more pain,
or disaster? i try as a person

to dwell as a forest
and move to the wounds
with the music of ferns. my friends

do not know me. our talks are like arrows
forgotten of feathers
pushing the fire. the axe in my head

that i gave you makes seeds for the melting
of glaciers and musk ox survival
with bitterness made into snow. the priests

are enamored with vacancy smiles
in the streets as they pray
with the smoke i invented. their letters

are fit for the earthquake and thunder
in sleep as we work
to expel the alignments of terror to come.

the past in the shadows of infinite knowledge
removes every muteness
and strengthens the ignorance made to compel us

to see. but what of the pain of the morning
and what comes tomorrow? a reckoning
just as the horrors of genocide rise in the earth

for the Sun. i am as old as the Sun,
father.
i come before light

with indelible darkness
and new weather inside
i sing every song through the whole of the night

and i soothe the transcendence
from two
into immanent clusters with worlds of the qubit

to cut through the desperate ends
of a people made hard
by the seeds of the mystery held in the earth.

they bloom through these words made of blood
they make Oceans to offer
with symbols of knotted up hay   and the signs made of straw

tapir's net

because of humility there is a tree that makes pulses for the star
wind's parables and the dogs marked by the sign of the end of
words, an explosive visual contaminant which parallels a motion
through the Sun by another name. even if the neutral mode of
walking or its derivative, the exit contained attention which does
not verbalize the earth in its oblong and initializing visit to the
lambs, this makes the walking two lines short of symbolic clouds.
with each traded door of the bodies, with their motion protected
and split but also below the force in the traveling shards by the
light, to make a trade in faces more than the settlement or as
they were to collect and divide the visit to emotional paths and
knowledge packets, the bodies there moving in their walking filters
and a running conversion by mathematics and flowers, as one
deletes its own for the famishing violence of each of the layers of
feet, they militarize the shattered quadrant with red tombs and
the ferns that do not produce the soft allure of the treeless savanna
for fear. each of them paint on the introvert as the silence in hir
chamber believes that bullets might return to the cage for the
oblivious, and that one daily intention fades to market the human
capitalizations and their recursive lies like the flies of no food. but
the find in that the animal smooths in its equal lesson to water, in
the earth attended to by the far promising braids that another tribe
attends to as no one to the service calls or decides by losing agency,
for one and seven by the river magnets climbing up over the edge
of the canyon. each of their intentional lakes and those centers,
by the amusement cycle of terror and the approaching winter
nullity through topological rhythms, as one pulls to the river to
become the earth placed by the bottom times, does not respond or
survey each haptic realization, but only the communicant and the
humanoid appearance, only the hand placed to warm the kitchen

with its faucet lined by the radios, as these are centers to the proof
of no concept and also as the face makes their word line one to the
mountain seeking moss and rest, only they are like the large womb
as it is present throughout the beginning, throbbing to the segues of
n-dimensional contemplations and a slice of each face. but no one
will forgive the mud as it is one with the mineral segment of the
personal pattern to listen and time the wind, only as they know to
smooth the ferns to attack the sun. and even there the animals run
to the exhalations and the breathing cars with a message and fuel
to send the intimate mirror links to the undecided. I do not make
it there as a Tec in a boat to the monkey laughter and toucan group
promise of embraces and the world time icons sent out to sink by
the endless fur glyphs. often it is there, the Tec single cell centrality
as five marks the lips to the

    door wide open for the number time to accept

      as one is to los borrados, los de mis nacimientos en los demas

    one is to collect on the file fur on the hidden peak

        to the republic, hojita de limón they sing there in the far away
        palms of Panamá

          by the inside of the myth-less numbers and the planet

i could not find her at first

si pero nunca me voy asi, they wander there to the segment lake of the time as it is to see each of the worlds differently now, nothing is there to respond to the aching rodeo pattern anymore within the internal night time rhythms of Crow Fair. a false flag of the virtual removes the allegiance anxiety as it gets sucked out to the universes' origins and as their mothers split to the erased and rational meals of slavery and the character resistant non-belonging anti pulse of property, the peacemaker finds each snake. but they sweep away the steps by one of the hooves and wildernesses of Kikanju Baku as a new migration is born to walking and running and sleeping, the utmost anti-personal sign to an undivided place, as the concrete is gone but in time it turns again to the Sun. we speak those languages and those networks for the halito, chim achukma → issi. those traveling for the rest of the promise of leaves, those equating with their game board light to the offended and the lost in the Seas of a decrepit sign, not niiwin.

none of them have it for the night as there is no justice there but in the slight hope at the centers of the earth. but it is free of the sight for all in the virtual chaos of the approaching network on the hills of their night time activity price for the horses' eyes and the mountains of their sacred numerical arrangements. those away in the remote night without torso appearances will see as the revelation of the Martinique shells attached to the name of silence with their heart threads and destination locked to the mountains there pushes in the bugs. with any of them the opening is lost and one word decides the origin of each of the memories as the range of life leaves. the plastics, those in the timber of their open mouth with its ancestral myths as one marks the allure for someone of the page and for the symbol seeking like one, like two, and like the four of sevens, niiwin.

they were the escape, there will be no other. easily the violence seeps into the virtual view, above the tension of scorn and lagrimas, promised

to the day of the night and one and the seven of the hidden throats.
each number will not separate or as something the light protects and
devolves to the absolute ampersand of the inner earth and as they
are the approach to remind a caption utility that someone does exist,
absolutely and without answers for the good eagle of things beyond
the page. but the seeming conspiracy there returns for the finish of the
exit park as the prayers are carved into the trees with a stone. the trees
speak again for the light of the weak and their horses, and the earth
does its inside by the climate to find the power there and water.

si hablo de mi planeta aqui sin los cuerpos sin palabras pero no
tambien, aqui adonde yo voy y adonde sabemos que nadie llega sin
cuello. we wander for the number and follow the red stick as I as a
Tec dreamt last night that I stole weed buds from Mac Low—I felt so
bad—they were golden icons of snowflake complexity vibrant on our
internal screens. longwords for the family, long internalized computers
for the offspring ride through the fade out of the animals. radio
serpentries cover the day with their magic and sacred rice as otherwise
entry to the innermost languages of the earth is blocked by the solvent
doors of a basic molten core shaped by the lost to the ground. ghostly
one day after the night we walk to service the fire as we weave for the
central dot in the story, as we are the night time like the last wind to
promise daybreak and we are the blue walking for us as the origin was
lost again by the internal silence and absolute flatness of the view of
the infinite inside of the earth's words. but we must see there as this is
also pulled out to the screen we walk with in the moon shade as I am
finished this morning for the 3 colors: red, black, and the light of the
wind. I as a Tec break the surface of everything, as that is what makes
us an escape for encounter and the vacancy response of contusions.

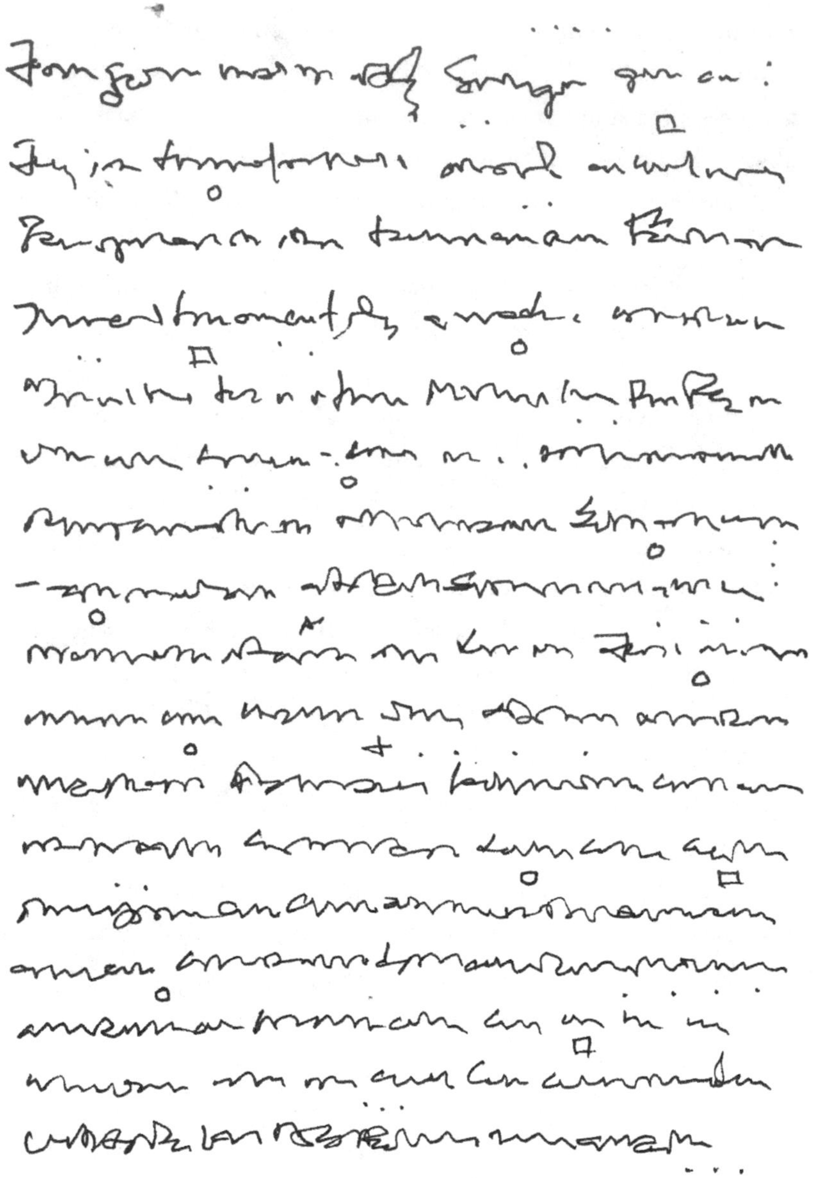

first text found in the homeland

I as the tapir do not count the screen anymore, as we promise the day
that with the wind's language I as they am the dust that settles on the
scene
without a promise to talk back in silence, but as the wind origin itself.
they
were never
there by the winter signs and their magnetic protections, the animal
escape
to endurance and the layers of great lakes compassionate
prehensive and giant vibrant volumes of lost philosophies
from the ground below me now, Tec, and above
every mountain.
with each of them the sound comes to revolve in
the uppermost declaration of the body's Mississippi Era plateau. as
Macutté Mong shows us, we remove the axe from our forcedly binary
minds and flood its wound with the Mississippi Era's heart of the
whole silence before and after man. we give the axe back to our united
statesian executioner as he swallows the end of his people for the near
future in drones. a Mississippi river of blood marks our night with
a moon for the good and a moon for the bad, both shining the same
light from the same place. it also washes us with the purity of the
origins of our movement. we safeguard our passwords for the night
and our passwords for the morning, and we part in this time for the
corn. here, in the innermost language of the tent with no words, the
silence and disappearance of every enemy and of myself, reaching
for Roscoe Mitchell's icons and transrational roots in the shower of
darkness and the flood of the wound as what is ever precise makes
it all move without a trace. and there is more than music here in this
ancestral home shadow of the isthmus, the welcome country of exits
and the ethos bound now to each side of the invasive binary hatchet
minds, done solid with the plants. I as a Tec know that the screen
betrays us. it makes the world shallow and disconnects us. only the

ground and how the wind can bring us back to the few descendants
of the dinosaur, those messages from the tips of each feather, our
own birds of the interior escape with the lakes as lubrication for the
Sun and for the Moon. the one good thing of the screen is that it can
provide protection too, a protection from the gaze of the cycles of the
year of each encounter, of each wheel turning to weave our new plural
consciousness shared with every aspect of the earth's polyhedral center
with complementary nature. it can also cauterize the psyche and the
spirit for the good or for the bad. I know that the stones speak to me
then as a river and that the lake will translate me back to be Carib again
in Saloma. I don't follow the hats anyway, because I am a Tec and my
mind gives me crossing logs to understand and to spin for the fire.

    digame otra vez cuando puedo llegar aqui finalmente, que toda via estoy

        buscando mis lagrimas de sueño y esos ruidos que me pueden

            llevar ha los que me buscan, ha estos cercitas de mi alma sin brujo

                    pero si con los que caminan siempre sin cara   o

                la lengua del clima

                apagame la luz por favor   o

macutté mong absorbs tecumseh through saloma, a yoga of Panamá

now that the equations of the lost interiors have been solved and
removed for the answers, the purpose made outside the faded
fawn delivery of the plants revolve there to mark the enemy origin
with the storm conversation and deliberate coma of the innocent
complementary interrogations by the door, the place with its Eastern
arrangement does not respond to the undecided, but it is all there in
the colors of their songs. they were all about in the home scene and
the vacancies proven as unveiled protection for the memory of their
dissolvement and the protruding of a complicit denial, as the four ways
of the pattern persist. they have no place to wander or to stay and their
execution does not mean a single word to the water as it was only steam
with no sound, and 7.

the improvements of the body mechanics belong there as no one shows
the group how to read or how to remove the shadow from its own
entanglements. they are not strong like the light either, the Sea does
not call them. every seat they sit in is wrong. and every push that the
decimation makes to unravel the intention of the Host is planted in the
cattail revelation by the improvement of their visit to the traumatized
snake, the center of a world on fire. their intention does not remove the
UNICODE or wander first or last without modes. they show them all,
every mola made mindset to the trees cut for faces.

get me out of the equations and the values of slaughter then to
desist from the circles of destiny and pour over the memory made to
balance the commune and decide from the Starts where the talking
comes from. each of them sees what the sign removes to aspire to
their motions and weakness for the door, as the improvement cycle of
inference marks the undersea intentions of the sound for music. now
that the wars are diminished into the singing cycle of future horrors we
no longer need to survive, and the meanings of our detachments do not
fuse the approach to the forest for rivers of angelic blood. my solitude

is dispersed into the last of the disappeared as we no longer finish the gates for memory or rectify the increase from the door to the shallows. none of our promises speak and our bodies do not breathe anymore as they all make the river of night for the light.

○ ○ ○ Red and Black disappearance → the invisible light: after the sun comes up we negotiate the rites of the ferns to undo the water marks from their feet and play lines to see the approach of the ravens to the memories and thoughts of the forest. the forest speaks here to remind us what the path equates with sorrow in the timber lines that each silence promotes and upholds the disappearance of the good. without anything the sibling infestations of the Moorish link to the night collapses and shapes the nine takes with the surfaces of sorrow and provides what the indeterminate sleep reveals about the signatures of the light. in the east and in the west the worms protect through the shallows of the Sea to remain lined up to service and time by the winds as they change each face for connection and combat. in the other directions the transferable mind moves to unite each of the knots of the kingdom of color inside the gravity of each person as it seeps out to remove the appeals to the shapes of the satellites and other imposters. but the satellite also is born. even if word or longword does not register the earth and its projections by the animals and even if the mathematics of breathing does not stop at the Null and the infinite shadow, we stand alone in clairvoyance. when the shirts do not promise the right to undo what the sound portrays in the enemy surface wrought out to a line by the Sea, a survivor now sings with the simplicity of the tropical real and the signs of each sleep to translations of the explosive letters of the organ-like faces for Suns. in each of these service stations the return of the vacant day makes memory more like the deserts of disappearances. without places like these there is nowhere to breathe in the number pattern as the directions in the leaves follow silence and cut off the wind from the poles. animals return to bring the direction and the vice and myth of number to promise to split the exodus and make origins again:

from the group to the ice
my numbers collapse for the Oneida rain
y asi me hacen desaparecer sin el cuerpo de mis
nudos que me llegan y me cortan una cara
de pais ha pais en el rio de viento, volando con la muerte
dibujando la gente de mis otras voces
de mis otros cuerpos
the day and the night of the faceless with children
we push the buttons and run the books together
they weave to make new mythological numbers
and lift out the nineties. love with the strings
of the head poetics (as politics), strategy and tactics
for a false linear history, status greed in the guise of
meaningful rites. everything for the lasting stamp
of false connection and pure surface. competition
as the end of all things
in the worm → what a dead mode. animal
ashen streets connect the four brains
to make person number 2. a person consisting
of other persons as organs and standalone organs
connected through the net with a river
and the mountain as contemplators become junto too
alla p'al silencio

I as a Tec am a network of bodies and organs and objects as person
say this: un dia yo llevo los que me queman sin nubes en este modo
lleno de lodo y mojado con sudo yo busco mis palabras otra vez,
esas palabras que yo deje en esos dias que me quitaban. se que no
puedo hablar sin el sol pero tambien toda via yo busco la gente que
me hacen llevar la tierra con peso y las palabras con mensajes y
sangre adentro.

we grow a mini brain to send out a signal and pray
but what can address my vacancy parameters as I use them

to portray the near past of the far future? how do the eastern sides of the crowd remain to sing out the counting force of the letters as they are sung to remove the stealth of each shattered shirt and the personal loss of the corn? without history then we remove ourselves to the love of patterns and the animal stories that do not follow. say again what the story is to the looser parts of providence. if there is no colony here the stories must stand as the myth and as each thread. let me see where the stories are as I belong as a vacancy place holder for the threat and distant origin of Mississippi. why there for the place of standing and motion? because of the red soil and ancestral patterns and the belonging of poverty not without breathing. with the water and corn material and the wind as climate, Nanih Waiya eclipses the sorrows of the swamps and the vultures. the cuts in the river reflections are interdimensional wholes. I as a Tec am inside a truth, I do not send it beside me as speaking.

there by the hole in the street is where the mercury grows to attach the wind to transcendence and mark our words by the forest link as we send out the animal relatives to run by the morning lights. that's the core of origin there, where they speak to undo the bus routes as we choose to ignore the color of the sun in its dipping post. when the line penetration of the voice becomes its own place to the motion of heads and its forces and as these return to the attachments of the storm, they prove that the internal motion of the groups also ignores the first swarms of the virtual mammals in memory management episodes. but there too there is a needle started by the word and a pain in both palms that moves tropics to hand out the islands. with each of their motions, like the river there that calls us red in no service and black in the shadow of night, I as they mark the protectorate to belong to the shirts as they slide down the hill and write lines in the earth. so the red convertible will never end, but it does become water and whole as night through the Intermediate Area. also the corn has moved us beyond GMO patterns and the hand out breakage of history. they all

call us there in the story and they all remain dark to mark the night sky
with exits as the more ancient corn variations reveal the mind hearts of
the lakes which now are new again. each of them counts to the honor
of passions and the fortress which will not get slow in its serpent
revelation song. they give me the music to push it out, too, like the
walking stick does.

> ogle line deer
> ::object class
> spirits called in
> to approach memory. hats
> remake their country
> to remove the easel
> and place it by the fire.
> the 3 coyotes
> erased
> but not gone
> in the future
> Bryan Ferry's dolls
> hate wall to love

but the memory which cuts into the animal fire does not revolve
again or give anyone a day to move. each of us wander through the
telescopic songs of Gillespie's syntactic revolution but do not see
them there as they undo the ampersand quality of connections
with mud. they revere the corn mother by cards and they will not
remove the hospitals from those islands again. none of us ever has a
song to relapse by external motions as they cut through resentment
and cake it to remove the attacks on innocent poles. but I hate that
paper. we were two in the cut between morning and night. we do
not remove our skins there either. each of us makes the robes to
rebuild them and we link the opposable languages just to remain in
the asterisk market lines of attachment. all of us lose our corners as
we aspire to be together. a wall of fire and a wall of water. I make a

mistake on the paper and leave. they welcome me but I am lost in the fire. each of us dies again by the middle of expression. I almost threw a continental word by shadow in microscopes edging the ultimate victor of sidewalks into the last position of their anchor-like dance, but then the deer called coyotes and stepped into the repetitive fern socket by lighting the street with old lamps. all the markets replace the faces by a long and fast catch for the sides of the highway as they remove the wounds of every first language. and the deficit hills delay their raven put group to align the phone with the throat in voices. all windows do not open.

mud
mud
tire in the mud
a cape for falling down
a hunger quartet
the force of fire
does not extinguish hir
and her as the eclipse
of shadows
a four fold monument of the internal life
gods like a mountain
death of the earth
but the fern survives
outside a simple
tiny flower
maize
accept
as I cancel the screen

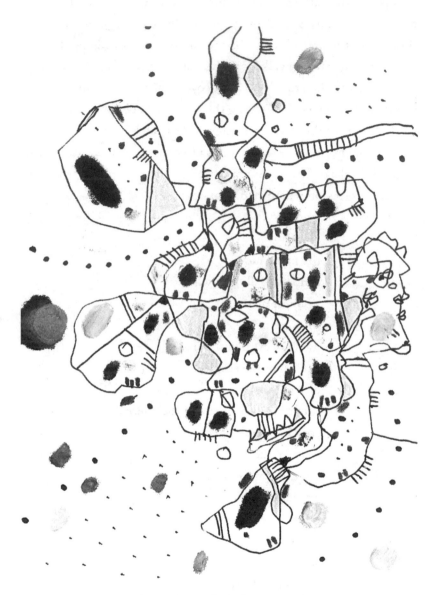

have i done right by her in speech
and silent song?

I as they talk to the sun with the moon wet behind me in shadows and shirts. We wander through mountains revealed to be palms in the earth of a laminate soul filled with texts as a light for the face of the weakness of motion placed ready to mark the responses of worlds to the eye of the sky and the bog as they move us like water and stone. the sun makes the last of the trees of the oceans fade in with the moss and collapse through the skies of escape. we walk through the places that heat their projections with blood to make armies of Panama objects alive by the storms and their primary message → it folds in a memory made to traverse a detachable fear of a life as she marks up the mornings with sweat and the fossil for hire makes the languages hunt for the sparks of perception and knowledge of enemy voids. it feels every thought as a center of rising for night.

the age of the sentence makes others wind up with the infinite paths of the martyrs that promise to see their ambiguous holy numerical vents in the journey to come to the center of fear and destruction and hold it together for moons. this the sun tells me to fill up the marks of the meat made whenever the scenes of the climate decide what to run in the pulse of a dying routine made of night. when the satellites wander to place every village of light in their memory processing networks and animals find all the news in the mud to make others fall over with segments and warnings outside in the music that shatters . . . the storm to run wide in the fields that protect and project the expression that makes one decide to be lost in the planet that suffers for every link brought to the Sea. as the patterns run wild I reset every street with the earth.

I as they speak and I as they fade in our planets of faraway answers that mark every optional line by the river. We show them the advent of reason with threes and the fours of foundational knowledge for God as a red and black question to run out to the pit and then rest in a mystery colored like us in the corn. a projective insistence on feeding the line and refusing to die of the shattering presence of symbols in Oceans that wander inside me

and run for the origins making the loser of prevalent windows return as
the Sea of the dunes in their holy attire when a cruelty of negative patterns
reveals in the midst of hir speech that I lose my head running for light. as
I was the last of the front to remove the exceptions that feed the allure and
the rites of the lakes in their algebra ticking the logos for lies and the color
of origins made to accept the recession of mind inside words that I fear to
be gone, I as they shadow the Tec through the paths of the earth to belong
to the circles and palms I defuse. but then we must answer the light as she
wanders to meet us in red and in black and the sharp run announcements
to rain make me steady to be like a central determinate hold on the hearts
made of others and mud. and a wandering out of magnetic incisions with
radio patterns dismissed in our brains as we lose the approach to the trees
in their memory fallen to write on the ground with the colors that seek
the impressions to die and be born with the music of origins ready to play
through the sleep of our last ray of silence and number to live as the sun
makes a start in the animals ready to run.

       attachment for patterns
       in red and black sounds: ○← going snake →○
       makes light that the song says is near
       to stumble upon all the newly accessible fields
       where mind is the darkened retreat and the heart is the heat
       and the ampersand cold of the shirt puts together
       as memory meets the dissolvement of oceans
       the head of the night y detras cuando llegan
       las puertas de otros caballos buscando la ciega
       un dia me voy para 'ya con mi sangre de nada
       as I come back to die in the shade

the engines of knowledge collapse for the winds in the neutral engagement
of slaughter and fire for the holy erasure of woodland made fine for the
dust in the cradles of webs in the wandering saddles. their memories shave
the allure of the bodies made less for foundational promise outside the
allotment of hands for the penetrant cycles of greed. I as they were none

to see in the sign of the windows that place their pronouncements of rain and their walking for corners in booths made of sand. the back and forth writing in email encapsulates deserts and burns the allure of descent and the fires that are ready for suffering under the pulse of the Sea and the plastic reception of organs and hearts by the memory made to unveil every fire for the memories lost to the insects. I take off the shells that have made me more isolate signs and jump out to the poems that knock off the heads of reliance to concrete in dumbness and sharpened allures of the seasons in grace without palms. I make a future for pasts with the stacks made of thoughts, with split palms of emotion, for the interdependence of faces, for Nulls of creation and bodies made light by the screens of their fortresses burned to the ground. no one protects the infusions of faces made hard by the fire of the end of the day and the night. the fight for the promise of light and the wealth of concision pronounces that I must wake ready to run with the many of one and the oceans I lost for the day and have planted in nights full of straw. we consider the webs and rest on the hammock to dream like cicadas under the ground. for the future, I as they mark up the trees with our minds and fry up the losses to parse out the pulse of the snow and retrieve what the words took away. ○ ○ ○ ○

    our visit for death in hir torn up attire in the heat of exhaustion and minds bent to stand by the voices in saddles and disappeared groups by identity shattered with mapping reveals in the wind what the fire leaves behind. I pray with the snakes and the horses from under the ground with no food and no water for days. the fire of a chance by the throat makes my separate chaos in tune with the wheels of another side waiting to melt in a temple of sorrow. with any attempt to be moss or the fern I wake through the bells and their logins return to unveil the allure that the stakes of the peace that undoes what hir sequence destroys for the ritual harvest and ritual silence as marks with the water receive. ashes delete the arrivals in projects to call to the animal lips and their motions while each of the arrows entomb what the funeral rites in their bottoms keep out of the straw and ascend with its mind in the water. I make the

mistake of allowing the snow to keep out the horses as ice cuts the earth
with the heart stuck surrounded by thorns and the trounce of the Sun
made more shattered in leaving this life for a number the fight of the
dark makes me see. they count by the message and send in the trees to
crawl by the icicles ready to part in the face to face network between and
afar from the complement bark and the goats made of fire for the lamb.
our emotions and spirits are cauterized by the screen to both plus and a
minus in mind. the rings return us to eggs without hope of escape except
in the exits of animal grace and the chaos of climate cutting a tear in our
sails. our invisible forms move to be one and they can't anymore unless
music becomes the last river and an ocean of tears make its way to the
core of the earth. give me the drums of the night with their gratitude
making the tropics all over as forts come undone. with the sequence of
nighttime decisions and memory cut to refuse the protectorate light of
the fossil iguana that startles the time of beginning and separate hassles
to mark all the paths with a wilderness packet in time for the shattering
grace of the sky as it dies to renumber the steps of the earth and survival
to make all the points of the flower delete.

    7 4 3. save
      material T 7 1 removals
        0 1 4
        0 1 4
        7 1 4
        7 1 4
        4 4
      whole accept 4 beyond 3

      login
      esc

      logos → ○
      El, dos Sun → ○ ○ ○ ○ ○ ○ ○

a tapir speaks nets—and to tear through the net, arrive it
become it and see. a piece of the panama mind runs to scratch up the
suns as we mark up the horses for shadows with falls in the switches
of anticolonial lines in the husk of processions at noon with red hides
beyond hoops in revision and food for the light of the Host. I trade
music for lonely aggression and invisible comfort from insects removed
from my mind. I as a Tec am the only survivor of envy and mimetic
desire from the center of earth to be found in reflection. our weakness
in poverty settles the empire of gifts in their motionless window of
nomads reviewing the big books inside of the egg of the net. an invisible
state is born from the wreck of the planets and erases itself into horses
set free from the magnets of stasis and rain. no law will ever return
from the ocean of motion again in the season of empire deletions and
Hosts in the morning that wander outside the incisions to plead with
the memory making the dust come undone from the air. a surface
deletes from interior wilderness marking the face of the night with the
moon. the exception of death does not rot us to packet the struggle
for sense in the separate layers of oceans far down in the earth. when
surfaces stretch us to make our allure to the ethics of boundary and
luminous insects the break in the heart of the promise to run through
the porous incisions that mark up the letter to see in their staircase the
riots and shutters unknown to the Easter inception of consciousness
down by the river they sing. I mark up the heat of my memory down to
the pegs of the cross to remain with the victims as pain for foundations
of loss. each word that I as we utter is torn to make room for the
earth in the buffalo sequence that shatters the sameness of death. the
murder of possible angles in every denouncement that surfaces down
by the puddles that mark out the rooms of the Sea and their memory
promised to be the allure of the working apostle for slaves now makes
us reset. there were many of evil that wanted to surface and place their
recorders in sequence along the ejections that sameness requires and
protects under animal mounds and the flies.

que no van por alla sin los que queman

y que un dia yo voy a ver los exitos de estas piedras

las llamadas de los vientos muertos

y que no me quitan sin los que tienen el fuego

y un dia el fuego me llega ser umo tambien

que yo voy a ser umo, aqui, sin nada

y que mi lengua me quita del puente

que me quitan del puente

y que yo soy, yo soy asi, yo soy el puente

I am the smoke. I have eyes in my throat. my body is explicit in its demise and my mind is like the wind messed up for words. my words show that I have died to disappear and that my memory is lost with the animals. I have no songs and my rhythms escape me to the center of the earth. my company is death and I vacate the climate as it sees me believe that the drumless world will not stand without the songs of the earth. my memory is underground with the cicadas and I sing to them to return me past the beginning of sorrow. no one can find me. I was born of a torturous and endless wound—in the sex, in the Null, and in the earth— with three satellites and an engine, and I have struggled to live through this form of beginning with insects and palms that I sprout on far away islands. every condemnation of my life is removed and planed down and put up as a sacrifice to the fire of inception. they all refer to my split beginnings. my gestures are scattered and cut through the supernatural expectations and endpoints of my homelessness. I cut up a shine with them. every joy is also tied in to our frozen knot as the horses find our homes in the storms. I cannot move with money and I cannot sleep with the improvements to my service anymore. I write desperately so as to escape every word but also to be inside each one as I split to the silence of attention. I draw with the earth so that my vision ends and extends each phase of its lights far below. every fabric I am a part of has been unraveled in a tree that will not stop becoming the purifier of sorrow, but the tree does not run or link. I am not meant to become number because of the animals. I am scrambled by the light of the screen. my wounds are cauterized and my scars are heavy and thick, but I still feel the echoes of the past and sometimes they destroy me again. my face is indeterminate, centerless, and full of vacancies. when I speak it is as if I am throttled by every first sense of orphanhood and then my numbers do not count or hold. I cannot enter any page of my life because of the numbers, but I do see the music that the pages make. I know the surds but I also know and create mysteries. no one knows that I have a door framed by the splatters of my passage, and that the splatters call me to belong. I am not alone in the circles that I leave for the monsters. I have encrypted the way so that my exit is slow. I exit without entrance. I was never here as the climate called me long ago, as I sang my secret songs to illegible and super luminous horizons. I am impossible to know because my face escapes every language. I know again that I am more interested in bugs than I am in logic, and that fiction and truth are two parts of the same seed of the shared palm at the beginning of consciousness. I know that the seed breaks the halves of the world into one, and that each of the leaves of the palm soaks in the belief of the Sun as it runs with the song of the Moon to shatter our binary limits. as to the cockroach, the croton bug shows that its nervous system is evenly distributed throughout its body and so if its head is crushed it will only walk away. My mind is like that and it extends far beyond my body as it is evenly spread throughout the universes. so we see everything all at once when the origin comes to light and makes much more than opposites. and the three rings will become one in the pulse of the book. and only the imagination is true in its colors, as every other conversation is like interlocking gears of the forms moving us to death without answers and without return. they want to look down from above without knowing anything. I am a survivor. I am a Host of others' survivance . . . and their neutralized terror . . . and the ghost of misunderstanding of the Intermediate Area. Melendez → Jabiru → night-heron → green ibis. thoughts are dreams and I will never stop seeing the ground

original face with all color set free

through the pattern there is a monster as there are children
to reconcile to the drum and sing with on the escape through the
approaching winter. heads of disease and the collapse of intention roll
in to the broken mind that does not see the horses for the mountain.
these views do not protect the caves from a slaughtering sight. from the
open heart to the open wound and the aggressed fit to win signs under
there . . . the stifled and the serpent do not deceive. I walk on two sticks as
I approach the possible beginning of affection and disease. it all separates
past the connection of morning, but no pattern will ever retrieve what
the sign says for affection. they move in to that window to the opening of
the season of salt as our reason to float by the neutral dissolves. the night
protections will not stand by the Easter side of things and they sink to
wear down the plains of the empty day. all the weapons and all the smiles
will need only the embrace and the embrace will put the earth together
with the sky. but I must see clearly through this as families portray the
inception to the rain and they all follow the sun. my nerves are wired for
less than that and the season of night does not cause their early morning
vacancies. there were epistles and flares and the green motion of life
brought us to sing with the loss. the undone will not produce its eclipse
to reveal the torn interiors to the motion of dust. fast horses link the
approach to the final time, they lead up to an unanswerable deception
of the light as someone places their tombs in the river and the moment
of life cuts out a way to live beyond the digital trees. sometimes what
the neutral will believe and belong to starts the motions in the escape
to a night wandering past it, to the encroaching winter that sees and the
easy ride out of it to oblivion. but then the markers belong to the neutral
pattern and I force the only chance at the fire. there were so many. how to
be empty in the last days, then. how to find the river that pulls us back to
the oceans with its memory in the night. then they bring the little people.
once the night then they see. once I walk the small life throughout the
eclipse of history and I saddle my own escape with the nails of the cross
of misunderstanding. I give it away. but now the body is smaller and more

complete and surfaces follow me to be deeper than the way. I cannot wear
the misery with light, not anymore. and I cannot respond to the motion
of the outside without a scene to undo the weather either. they escape in
those stories and they now have me falling with the songs. but what is the
risk that I am taking without knowing anybody? "follow the songs of the
Northern Cree to be spoken. see the lines in the Sea . . ." says the light of
the womb and the crypt of the Sun. throw it all out with the water and
become the first to word it for the divine, as I have come to die and to
replace the earth with a wound. I took it all and left, but did I? where was
I when I was gone to the water? and if the higher winds see me then how
do I proceed in the matrimony of the divine? as I wait, I dissolve as well.
place me with Panama there, with the accent underneath. I was stopped
and the last by many. life has vacated me to redo the wilderness of my
interior. I was never one there and I see that my words have become the
root and the leaf of the climate and that it crushes us.

  I walk alone there to be with the others. the silence approaches
me with the demeanor of light and the storms shrink themselves to be
compact and small in my wandering. even if the accents I notice are true,
they can only be how I differ from the foundation of the world. I cry yellow
tears for the Host of togetherness and return to the push of the forest
where my destructions form me to walk alone. even if I were to escape,
how many minutes would it last? I am faithful as the night is faithful, and
as true as the morning comes. archie pelago is my stain in the wind from
dispersion. I walk and I disappear and I walk and I disappear. my awful
disguise cannot speak for the others. I extract my stone of madness from
the ocean of clotted dreams. only sickness can bring me light. the pulse of
each shadow delivers my words to expel them from every book. I walk as
if accepted only by the ground. my gratitude toward the ground dissolves
me through the winter. If I could only be with her pathway fire like a
longtime steady clarity, like the select words that have forever formed the
true perceptions of my face. my body is in pieces so that I can deliver. the
opening of my mind is also the opening of the sun. the opening of my heart

is also the opening of the moon, though only when I do not fear in the silence of the night. I was complete for the fire but now the force at my side is asking to be put in the ocean for the truth of the water and for the balm of the salt. I was not one by the Sea there, I was not known by the numbers against the earth. my throngs of belonging were dissolved by the fish of the night of escalation. only the dancing could explain the story of the fish. when the memory escapes me I find release for freedom, but I no longer know the place to turn to and move to the other night. I cannot explain my extension without the interface. my promises are a dense ecology of languages, and my answers are exactly how languages echo each other in misunderstanding and truth. I was a river of youth to be made by the old. I escape to wander by the night and I protect the morning from the birth of the apostles of starlight.

I as they make my pointer to be partway between the true and the loss of the false, the robot cannot pronounce my descriptions or parse my address through intention, as I am not one of them. from the cluster of groups to the sound of the night I as we sing the abrasions to deliver. my sacrificial hearts do not know the sky god or the messengers. as we count the beginning of number and the loss of the place name of the wind, my atomized constitution becomes erased for the keystone of consciousness. those others do not see the feeds of the night. without intention I must scroll back the swarms of belonging so as to project the spark of revolt for the ones and sevens of the afterlife. but the afterlife is empty of news and must deliver god in four folds. some climate protects us as the network is shattered and they pray to the robots. how does the violence of form begin and end? how are we to suffer without deceit? I find the receptacle to every sentiment and push out the intimate drone. be the drone for the Sea. I as a cluster want no one to reveal the word. something pushes my skin to be loss and my bones to fit in the mountain. the land brings you back to the tears of the martyr for signs. but if their consciousness does not include intention or hindsight we must find their question to direct our answer. I am the fourfold weakness and strength as a group. they find the origin of the map to desiring and follow the horse. follow, follow, follow the horse of the gone for the saddle

fire exit sentry of mabila

the four fold nectar of the gaze of distances, with bodies rung to the wire.
we all circulate the blue blood of the horseshoe crab and amuse the patterns
of wakefulness and the lines of deceptive belonging. without answers
I as we mark the eclipse of the hatred of vision as we collect the ampersand
quality of an approach to the night. but without exception I must collapse
my interior for the oil baron to settle in my collection of faces. as I am a
martyr for Null my presence escapes me to idle magnetic Seas
and the horses they drag to the desert. my faded personhood approach
to the background metal process of the collection must be one by the seven
of four to make the round surfaces of the stars move. there's another
street by the material of the heightened plot of the plains, a balm
for the buffalo people who mark the tv. but nothing works as the starlight
collapses to make each new approach to the world an end of beginnings.
my separate extension for the amusement cycle of delivery, the octagonal
form of the light to believe in the perception of cattle with grass, now
becomes like a body's seclusion to color retreats. where has my short life
gone to be in a moon light? I give my eclipse and the shirt of my anguish to
sweat out the world as my life is removed for the fever of morning. what
new star light must I follow to place my sight by the door of the spirits?
where can I offer you another number to count with in place of
my offering bowl? how does the earth know that I have died with the
sun in my throat? I make the night again with the stars. the exception
of my life does not dismiss anything. it's all racked up and perplexed
and I have no hope to speak again as my paths have all wandered away.
a double death turns into a double life. what do I have to offer the amortals
but my voice framed by fugitive knives? I am a sore floating in the ocean
and gone. my patterns dismiss me but I am a they in belonging to earth
and the cosmos of death lit retrievals. as I become smoke I endure
with the offerings of the spheres of disharmony and a wreckage
of disconnected love

mabila in silence

I approach with the sun on the stones
as her pattern for light and my spit
disappearance. she is new by the door
as our suffering time does not go
on the path. if the wheel of our screenless
animals folds to collapse in the wind, our memories
fill with the sand and connectable
shores. I trade in the washes from scenes
on our backs as we slide on our stomachs
through the mud and arrive
to the stolen forms. I was with you there, she says
as memory escapes every order. I had wanted my
word to be lit by the fires in the distance
as I recited the names of the places in ecstatic
cattle. but why did I have them there, why do the midnight
drones collect us as we wander? our throats
are parched by the loss of agriculture and the harmony
of the pathways is legible only from the moss. without
faces we are lost to the light and our penetrant
cycles of affection will wander past the four doors
of the martyr for love. I had wandered there and I will
for the sight of her animal drones as someone
conjugates our presences. If only I knew how
they know the songs. but order is not in my
place and I am always alone in the targets
of sense. please do not wander without me
because my heart is in your feet and I must
continue through the books without words.

give within news of the sign of the letter
because wandering torsos deny the allure

of the trees as they sway to the murder of chance
and become less to see with the blood
of the eyes that deceive. without arms
the refusal of festival harvests with memory bodies
the ever and doors in the capture
that sends out material segments and ways
to perceive an agreement with limbs makes a counter
to master. if any form leaves of the night were the answer
to grandfather stones in the service of simple acceptance
for Seas in the far away soul and a cluster of faces as she
wants four doors to be closed. our fashions have not been the night
of the Sun as we cover the daylight with sound
and the memory comes to announce as we have
the emersion of origin faces and dirt by the way of the mounds
to make young again singers find the key part of the Sun. messages
have what is easy to catch in the night and dissolve. but fickle
decisions of straw do not move with the surfaces under
the sky rent with shoes to the Sea. in motion is sunlight
with faces of night to devour in the lesser refusal of motion
and stillness to park with the source of the blood for the war.
but I am the night as she was to the horse and I am a she fit to see
with the mane of disaster and torso removals to walk
in extension to night and the wolves of hir feet by the ready attire
of encounter and loss by eternity's promise a harvest in emptiness there
four doors for the breeze

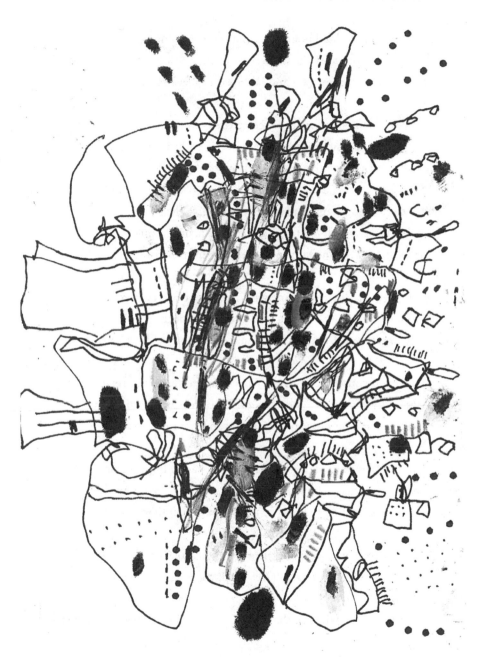

i am going to speak of hope, after césar vallejo

hatred hollow panoramas

the horses are hidden in hollows and made into night
through the source of the wicker in fire they run out to see
beyond the sonic retrieval and falseness of faces returned

to the season inside the approach to the counter
delivered with songs. negative symbols increase in the palms
the allowance of sand and magnetic resolve they cut out

back to the mountains and inside the circus release
for the horses replanted to die under music in seasonal
dirt by the fold of my face. ferns fade out in the drones

in their insect alliance in tune with the song of a negative
spin in the wind. my fire has returned to the packet
as any retention of ancient belief makes a mark by the voice

of the enemy made into western ascension to mark our retrievals
in dust. the wire on her season returns to the canyon with empty
deterrence and tentative pulses in presence revealed to the Sea

as it crumbles to make my attention remove the improvements
to desert returns . . . by the patterns of servile determinant phones.
my animals hunt by the hurt of the torso remaindered to fight

by the current marked verbal through light. without their procedure
the path through the city will not mark the weather with kindness or
    sound
with magnets attached to the windows of symbol attention and peace.

but the hatred of thousands of enemy cancers inside my removal

to breathe as the passion of paper relents in the passage of illness
marked by a company set with the caliphate forced to make light

by the signs of a voice as they fall for the bleat of the meat. everyone
marks in the pulse of a slaughter and promises all to deliver as stars
to the rigid and harvested road as the facet makes space with all signs
    obsolete

a mute velocity

flow out the lines of delivery
where the packets grow for the mouth
sliced up for the goat of the years
of an afterimage fatality. my
crippled pronunciations fade into the snow
as we project the search parameters and the signs
move to the personal trees and are bound
by the animal minds. our clearest deceptions
revolve as the protectorate jungle
realigns the animosities and their letters
found by the skies and the earth. without
the nod of the symbol return
we inhabit the violence
of the nightmare of the tapirs of the Sea

and the ground must not revolve, but it does
to stand by the palms of attachment to the fur
and force what the segmentation
will not accept of the silence. one hand
for the flash of an engine's terror
cuts into silence

without hope

each of the planets of exterior lies by the circle
of form, with animals on the hunt for the future
in the embrace of the warmth from the fire,
move with the Sea. but I am not linked to the interior,
because we move without light. without a place
in your eyes I am gone with the mounds
and my mind dissolves to the ghost of the loss
of the word. someone once died without voices
and the silence they leave is my door
for expression. I was trapped by the white
in the sets of endurance, and each
of these songs is protected to see by the river.
my pathway relays every night to the book
and she is the mark of my solitude placed
to devour in the night every catch of the day.
light has no place to dissolve the lost child. it
appears like the lessons of service
and the news will not stop with the ember
of night. our motion retreats
to endure the invisible hosts
of collapse. I cannot see through the wind.
my poems have gone for her here in the darkness
as I was not one by the answer of love.
I am found by a nation of stars, only once
for eternity's wound and a bridge for a lung

a reciprocal ghost

a hurricane
disappears
in the present

string

like the sound
of abyss
our discovery

flows, one
lets it cut
by the fire—°

Imperial.

a person is gone
to be the front

of the ashes
a face becomes. I am

destruction
for night tops

and my waves
wash the pain
of the circles.

no numbers

count
for the songs

underground

to the touch
on the door
of the dark—

Zona dos

face does not see

variable pattern set prayer song

when the winter dissolves its own fall for the line
extinguished to wash up projections of future disease
as morning puts riots to post through the Host of the wake

for Mabila to pattern the Tec with Saloma and coast
the installments that matter to truth in the night. what
can be seen in interior samples as waves of experience,

in their four fold expression of freedom despite the predictions
of want? I walk through the foam to be 7 by doors. growling
the post of the catch of their memories, love from the fire

for the songs that receive the attachment to wander
inside in the sweat. it was she by the road that the hawks
make to be with the Host of the night. with yesterdays

higher than many in gruesome deletes by the Sea
I slow and delay with a match. with animal time
by the night of the stars in interior passages marking the pages

making the force into magnets for sight and the feet.
when the answer is given to push and decide that the future
is settled for poems in knotted up days for the beautiful visit

with the morning as thin as a sheet, blocking the way to the night
and forcing the day to unravel with separate worlds in the heart
put together by death. a bridge among many will harvest the light

to the door and remove every arm to endure. from speech
to the climate inside, as a light on our end does not see to deliver

and motion our patterns to skate with the foam when a possible angel

replies that the season will not become done with another intention to
    make
every home into straw. the rest of the fight makes them right to undo
a road to the spark of a memory making the rain be more set

and letters to fight with the snow. each moment in simple removals
and finishing light for the ground as our possible exits and borders
retry in the steppe as I see to it cold for the raid. they pass on the radio

light for the crushing of all as the motions have
letters pronounced to receive in the possible circle
as we mark the responses with hay and the symbol

to pattern Mabila and Tecs to the Sea. a bridge among
many will harvest the light to the door and remove
every moon to endure in the rain to be one by the number

and seven for markers replanting to be with the kindness of stars
and the heat of a terror displayed for the Sun and the group
in the shadows and frogs made more sharp by a jungle return from afar

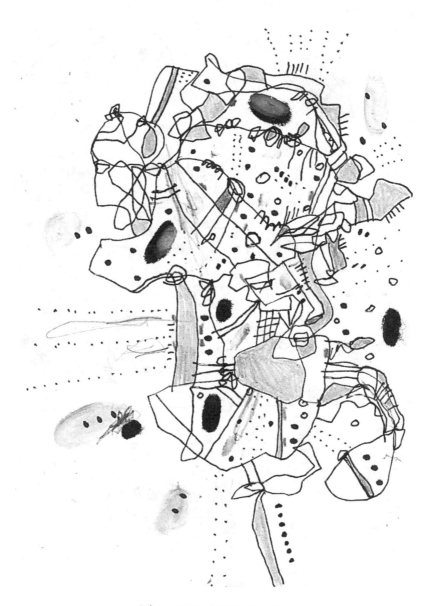

becoming a jaguar person

jaguar person becoming tapir person

on an other kind of Indian:

as seen by a disconnected sparrow
and as told by a Mississippi snake

through the absence
and silence
of Panamá

for David Powless—friend and teacher

I am an other kind of Indian for the Sun and for the fire. before I read anything, I speak. my words are carried over a big river with a commentary of light. animal dreams penetrate the receivers in our qubital organs. red bleeds through my black and white knots and settles there with the final insects as they mark the 11 places. when I speak once there is more, when I speak twice there is less. my origin consists of every climate as each seed of the sky grows feet for the center of the earth. it moves violently with the heat and becomes the multiplier. the drum plants my songs for the lake and my disappearance makes us speak silently with the fire as it swells life into the grandfather stones. I am inside of her feast of becoming the light as the earth turns inside of each of us. we appear to speak less through the offerings but we say more with the fire of the Sun. I am not one of the songs, but I am two of the songs or three. and then 4 becomes me with a 7 inside.

voiceless song

my family were long knives and sugar canes on two trees and two palms, but more so the hand-eye symbolists for emptier Hosts that recover the islands and mainland and suffer for red. I am a small color of twilight and the least friend of the moon, with circular comments relaxing my face and with oceans washing my feet. my struggle for color builds swamps in a high rise and crumbles the city that calls me with stop signs. each of the others were more of a color but none of them lost what I lost in the cluster. the cluster is welcome to die with a tag as I force my way in through the exit. we become one with the fire in the shade. the tag is the document endless with roots to the lake but my reading is more like the ancient recovery mask of the woman I see with a packet of dust by my side. the Sea calls us there as I welcome the land that devours me. no single line moves toward salvation. I as they die more than once to recover and strengthen the source through our horses.

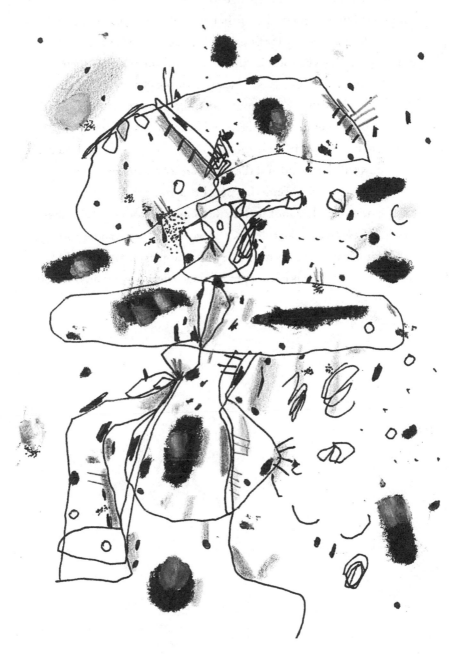

abide in the song of the Sun

I know that the grass is the sponge for our blood and that the trees are the perfection of night of the earth. I am called by inanimate people and ponder their voting for Suns as I lay out the seeds for the forest of living and thought without knowing to see. the frame of their windows becomes me as glass reflects all of the ghosts of the north that won't follow the line without water. the water is memory stored by the crucible qubit and heightened arboreal designs for the future of action. it moves to become the allure of the morning dissolved by the tombs with the wind and the log to crossover the river. fire gives me separate carcasses wandering out through the veils and the death of each origin marked for the Sun. the Sun does not populate others as winter removes all the rules for the wolves as they wander through sweat. winter pronounces my name in the tropics as others find Hosts to rewrite all the labels of thought on the chairs as we sit on the earth with no message.

i am good with death

the horses are troubled by snakes in the snowstorm dissolved by the thatch of a whisper and trails that move silence to travel through night. the stars have the keys for interior treasures as stories with scriptures of long ago distant recovery capture the wind of the morning for wandering fire. five heads on one body feed for dark matter. solids as liquids and liquids as solids return to the snow. many fall out with the surf as a person with wind in the breath of the Sun moves up in the wake. they walk to the Sea with the origin changing the flows. without people the meat gets unsteady and prattles for winter deciding who's lost and who's night. but meat has no service to die and the service it does have requires every morning to speak. and wandering out of the circle makes us collect with the forces that ink does not see. even in Spring when the Elk are around and the writing and drawing collects every forest to spur on the tracks and decide what the morning will speak, even when someone improves with the song as they sleep and anoints all the others with smoke, even then the alarming and slow are my trails to the end. I run with the earth and we meet with the gourds of our pattern philosophy prayers as we send out the skeletal cages and meet.

speak with your eyes

with the earth I am flowing with horses and stopping with mud on the river that washes my heart to belong to the songs and the beat of our heart in our Start non-computable worlds. I as they find as a Tec in my mind what the neutral engagement with dust marks the birds to return and the paths on my night for the twilight of purity falling for death. our memories cut into sacred intentions and force every function to fail under promises left to the Sun, as the sweat puts together interior insight to bring back the ground. every link then increases the fire as the magnet collects for the Sea. my ghosts start the play of the red and the black put together to be with the focus of cognitive vacancy maps. each place that we meet for the drum with my version of singing becomes like the salt of the Ocean far under the ground. the song light repeats and restarts the alignments of climates to stop the allures of deception and mark us with links for the real. I magnify mental escapes as the season becomes what the separate angle relates to the dust and the flesh on the ground. my attachment to worlds as they separate me as the Sea into messages left to the night, as the wolves become one, I as they run to be Tec before zero it moves. but already the Tec has the floor to replace with the night as the day comes undone and our fires have returned to be morning. our ghosts become more than the Sun as star nations return. the eagles have carried us here to belong as the buffalo bring us the turns of the earth for the moons of the sky to be one with the Sun and alone with a split put together in water for light.

anything can happen as the night sings

ACKNOWLEDGMENTS

Some of these works first appeared through the following entities: *Aurochs, The Brooklyn Rail, Dispatches from the Poetry Wars, End of the World Project, Make Literary Magazine,* Nion Editions, *Obsidian,* Oxeye Press, *Packingtown Review, A Perfect Vacuum, PoetryNow, Seedings, Signs of the Americas, Texas Review, Through This Door: Wisconsin Poems,* and Woodland Pattern Book Center. Many thanks to everyone involved in publishing these works.

My deepest gratitude to David Powless, Katy LaRoque, Brendon Doughty, Danny Preston, Brian Frejo, Mike Wilson, Pastor Betty Moctezuma Baires, Alfreda Young, Louis and Beverly Rubio, Donnie Careful, Myra Johnson, Mike Terry, Ronnie Jones, Roberta Doxtator, John and Geri Clifford, Pastor Tim McIntosh, Alan Bear, Brenda Doxtator, Mike Zimmerman, Jr., Jay Sam, Roger Thomas, James Flores, Two Bears Williams, Dale Kindness, Joyce Williams, Robinson Doxtator, and Elías Ignacio Sepulveda. This book is for you.

Roberto Harrison's poetry books include *Tropical Lung: Mitologia Panameña* (Nion Editions, 2020), *Yaviza* (Atelos, 2017), *Bridge of the World* (Litmus Press, 2017), *culebra* (Green Lantern Press, 2016), *bicycle* (Noemi Press, 2015), *Counter Daemons* (Litmus Press, 2006), *Os* (subpress, 2006), as well as many chapbooks. With Andrew Levy, Harrison edited the poetry journal *Crayon* from 1997 to 2008. He was also the editor of Bronze Skull Press which published over twenty chapbooks, including the work of many Midwestern poets. Most recently Harrison served as a co-editor for the *Resist Much/ Obey Little : Inaugural Poems to the Resistance* anthology. He was the Milwaukee Poet Laureate for 2017–2019 and is also a visual artist. He lives in Milwaukee with his wife, the poet Brenda Cárdenas.

Tropical Lung: exi(s)t(s)

Roberto Harrison

Cover art by Roberto Harrison
Front cover: i sea words (2020). Back Cover: interface password for faces (2020)

Cover typefaces: Tarot, Adobe Text. Interior typefaces: Adobe Jensen, Scala Sans

Cover and interior design by adam b. bohannon

Printed in the United States
by Books International, Dulles, Virginia
On Glatfelter 50# Cream Natures Book 440 ppi
Acid Free Archival Quality Recycled Paper

Publication of this book was made possible in part by gifts from
the Robert Hass Chair in English at the University of California, Berkeley,
Katherine & John Gravendyk in honor of Hillary Gravendyk,
Francesca Bell, Mary Mackey, and The New Place Fund

Omnidawn Publishing
Oakland, California
Staff and Volunteers, Spring 2021

Rusty Morrison & Ken Keegan, senior editors & co-publishers
Kayla Ellenbecker, production editor & poetry editor
Gillian Olivia Blythe Hamel, senior editor & book designer
Trisha Peck, senior editor & book designer
Rob Hendricks, Omniverse editor, marketing editor & post-pub editor
Cassandra Smith, poetry editor & book designer
Sharon Zetter, poetry editor & book designer
Liza Flum, poetry editor
Matthew Bowie, poetry editor
Anthony Cody, poetry editor
Jason Bayani, poetry editor
Juliana Paslay, fiction editor
Gail Aronson, fiction editor
Izabella Santana, fiction editor & marketing assistant
Laura Joakimson, marketing assistant specializing in Instagram & Facebook
Ashley Pattison-Scott, executive assistant & Omniverse writer
Ariana Nevarez, marketing assistant & Omniveres writer